Wicca Magic

A HANDBOOK OF WICCAN HISTORY, TRADITIONS, AND RITUALS

AGNES HOLLYHOCK

wellfleet
press

© 2023 by Quarto Publishing Group USA Inc.

First published in 2023 by Wellfleet Press,
an imprint of The Quarto Group,
142 West 36th Street, 4th Floor,
New York, NY 10018, USA
T (212) 779-4972 F (212) 779-6058
www.Quarto.com

Wellfleet titles are also available at discount for retail, wholesale, promotional, and bulk purchase. For details, contact the Special Sales Manager by email at specialsales@quarto.com or by mail at The Quarto Group, Attn: Special Sales Manager, 100 Cummings Center Suite 265D, Beverly, MA 01915 USA.

10 9 8 7 6 5 4 3 2 1

ISBN: 978-1-57715-396-2

Library of Congress Cataloging-in-Publication Data

Names: Hollyhock, Agnes, author.
Title: Wicca magic : a handbook of Wiccan history, traditions, and rituals
  / Agnes Hollyhock.
Description: New York, NY, USA : Wellfleet Press, 2023. | Series: Mystical
  handbook ; 17 | Includes bibliographical references and index. |
  Summary: "Wicca Magic is the essential introduction to this ancient
  practice that features the history of the craft alongside practical
  magic, rituals, and spells to harness positive intentions that conjure
  self-discovery, peace, love, and abundance into your life"-- Provided by
  publisher.
Identifiers: LCCN 2023016712 (print) | LCCN 2023016713 (ebook) | ISBN
  9781577153962 | ISBN 9780760385579 (ebook)
Subjects: LCSH: Wicca. | Magic. | Witchcraft.
Classification: LCC BP605.W53 H65 2023 (print) | LCC BP605.W53 (ebook) |
  DDC 299/.942--dc23/eng/20230509
LC record available at https://lccn.loc.gov/2023016712
LC ebook record available at https://lccn.loc.gov/2023016713

Publisher: Rage Kindelsperger
Creative Director: Laura Drew
Editorial Director: Erin Canning
Managing Editor: Cara Donaldson
Editor: Amy Lyons
Cover Design: Beth Middleworth
Layout Design: Ashely Prine

Printed in China

Contents

Introduction

✳ · ○ —— ○ · ✳

Welcome seeker and merry meet!

You hold in your hands an open door to the practice of Wicca. In a solitary practice, the Goddess and God will commune to you in whatever way they see fit and, in turn, you'll carve out your own craft as you learn and grow. Practicing is the most important part of Wicca, and the best way to do that is just to start. The frameworks for esabats, sabbats, altars, rituals, and much more are provided within these pages. Pathways will be pointed to, and it is your choice how you'd like to pursue them. This gentle framework is meant to help eclectic Wiccans practice in isolation, although the guidance here could bolster an individual's practice in tandem with a coven.

We create the most praise for the Gods by learning and growing. The beliefs, practices, rituals, and ceremonial structure share a common root in all Wiccans, but your relationship with the Gods will be deeply intimate and personal. The right way to cast a circle and the names of the Divine differ between lineages and even from coven to coven. There are many ways to honor the God and Goddess, and it is not my place to judge what is right or what is wrong. The uniting factor between all Wiccans is that we practice, and there is no fundamentally right or wrong way to do so. Venerate the powers that be and make the magic happen.

Thus, open your heart. Hear the call of the Mother, succumb to the dance of the Maiden, behoove the wisdom of the Crone, and fall into flank with the wild hunt. Most of all, listen to that primal voice in your heart. Fold Wicca into your life in little ways, and you will clasp the hands of the God and Goddess.

Shall we begin?

History and Structure of Wicca

To know where you're going, you must know the paths walked by those before us. History is an important part in unfolding the mysteries of Wicca. The roots run deep, and the lore is littered with wild hunters. Begin at the beginning for the loose origins, structure, and language of Wicca.

What Is Wicca?

Witchcraft and Wicca are often conflated, and while a Wiccan may practice witchcraft, Wicca is something unique. Wicca is a neo-pagan, ritualistic, natural religion that has been developing in its current form since the 1950s. It is based on an amalgamation of pre-Christian pagan beliefs and practices and ceremonial magics from esoteric secret societies.

Sometimes Wicca is called "the old religion" because its roots are in the anthropological search for pre-Christian practices. *Paganism*, another term used to describe Wiccans, comes from the Latin word for "rural" or "rustic." Christians in the Roman Empire labeled all the country citizens practicing folk religions as pagans. Many pagan beliefs (often expressed through oral tradition and passed down through family ties) were lost as Christianity supplanted local belief systems.

Neo-pagan beliefs are attempts to harken back to these lost roots. Neo-paganism emerged with the spiritualist movement in the 1900s and is still going strong today. Many neo-pagan practices, including Wicca, are nature-based religions that seek harmony with the natural world. Rituals and ceremonies honor the cycle of the seasons, the movement of the stars, and the changes in the moon, and the mythology of the Divine reflects this.

Wicca is also a mystery religion, meaning that, in most cases, you must be initiated into it and take an oath of secrecy to protect the mysteries of the craft. No one is born Wiccan, even if they have Wiccan parents.

Additionally, there are many different lineages and traditions of Wiccans. Despite their differences, the connective tissue among the different branches of Wicca is a consistent religious practice, respect for nature, and reverence of the Goddess and God.

WICCA, WICCANS, WITCHES, AND WITCHCRAFT

Wicca's original spelling was Wica. It is said that the Old Religion called some of the practices of Wicca "the craft of the wise," which evolved into "witchcraft" over time. The first time the word Wicca was used was in the 1960s, well after the religion had begun gaining popularity. Witchcraft is the practice of using spells, visualizations, and magic to bring desired outcomes into reality. Wicca is a religion that utilizes elements of witchcraft. Capitalizing Witchcraft likens it to Wicca and changes its meaning from something that is practiced into a fully structured religion. Lowercase witchcraft is the practice of magic and does not need to be tied to a religion to be experienced. Some Wiccans practice Wicca, but not witchcraft. Alternatively, many religions practice magic without being Wicca.

History and Important Figures

As Western esotericism began to develop with the repeal of laws prohibiting witchcraft, covens with diverse beliefs and practices began to emerge and spread from the United Kingdom to the United States. Knowing where Wicca started can help young Wiccans figure out where they want to go.

MURRAY, GARDNER, AND WICCA'S FOUNDING

Wicca as we know it today has its roots in the 1920s when Margaret Murray published her book *The Witch Cult of Eastern Europe* and made anthropological arguments that suggested there was an unbroken line of covens practicing witchcraft in secret from pre-Christian times. While Murray's theory has since been academically disproved, her work provided the seed of Wicca that Gerald Gardner watered in the 1950s and 1960s.

Gerald Gardner can be a bit of a controversial figure, but he is indisputably an important person in neo-pagan occultist history and in Wicca. Gardner had a background in Freemasonry and connections to the Hermetic Order of the Golden Dawn, and many of the practices in Wicca look very similar to the ceremonial practices of these institutions.

Along with the guidance of Doreen Valiente, Alexander Sanders, and other foundational members of the coven, ritual practices and the veneration of two prime deities (a divine feminine Goddess

of the moon and earth and a divine masculine horned God of the hunt and death) were the foundation of what Wicca is today.

⚬⟶ HIGH PRIESTESS ⟵⚬
DOREEN VALIENTE

If Gerald Gardner is the father of modern-day Wicca, then Doreen Valiente is certainly the mother. High Priestess of the Bricket Wood Coven, Valiente was responsible for fine-tuning language and ritual practices crafted by Gardner. She fractured from original Gardnerian Wicca in its early days (before it was even called Wicca) and continued to teach the ways of Wicca.

Valiente's works are seminal to Wicca, and if you're pioneering your own home brew brand of Wicca, seeking out the works of Valiente for inspiration and guidance is a must.

MAGIC OR MAGICK?

The inclusion of a k in magick emerged to differentiate between occult magic—like Wicca—and stage magic—like that of Harry Houdini. If you wrote about magick in the 1920s, you were speaking of it in a spiritual sense. Different styles and lineages may add the k, while others forgo it. This is completely at the discretion of the witch, and in this book, magic will be written without the k.

EARLY ISSUES AND MODERN PRACTICES

Aside from the lack of scholarly validity in Murray's original witch cult hypothesis, there were other issues in Wicca's inception worth mentioning. Many foundational occultists were homophobic and misogynistic. Needless to say, this doesn't quite align with the population that Wicca and witchcraft appeals to today. As Wicca developed, people like Doreen Valiente checked some of Gardner's attempts at instilling patriarchal and misogynistic values into Wicca. The Minoan Brotherhood took the bones of Wicca and created a coven exclusively for gay men. These practices do not absolve Gardner and others for their behavior. Rather, it illuminates how Wicca has evolved past the desires of their founders.

Lineages and Traditions

As the ideas behind Wicca grew, but the practices of coven mates diverged, different lineages and traditions began to emerge. A lineage is how Wiccans trace back the line of their practices to an influential founder. For example, a modern-day Gardnerian coven can trace their lineage through High Priestesses or High Priests back to Gerald Gardner's first established coven, the Bricket Wood Coven.

Different lineages hold different beliefs and pass on the secret mysteries of their religion to their initiates. Initiation is a ritual where an individual dedicates themselves to the God and Goddess and swears an oath of secrecy to keep the mysteries of their coven close to their chest. Lineages also frequently copy down a coven Book of Shadows to ensure the secrets of their tradition are not lost. People of the same lineage share beliefs and ritual methodologies and participate in a network of knowledge with other Wiccans of their lineage.

What follows is by no means an exhaustive list of different Wiccan lineages available to you, but rather a baseline to begin your search.

GARDNERIAN WICCA Also called British Traditional Wicca (BTW). When people think of Wicca, Gardnerian is usually the lineage that comes to mind. Covens that practice Gardnerian Wicca can trace their lineage back to Gerald Gardner. In spite of their common origin, current Gardnerian practices are still quite diverse. Gardnerian Wiccan practices are ceremonial, with specific chants, invocations, and rituals that are passed down with minimal deviations.

DIANIC WICCA Dianic Wicca is heavily focused on the Goddess and often excludes the God entirely. This mythology is tied to the Roman Goddess of the moon, Diana, and some of the foundational practices are loosely based on Italian folklore and Charles Leland's *Aradia: The Gospel of Witches*.

CELTIC WICCA Half of the Wheel of the Year celebrations (see page 52) are derived from ancient Celtic fire festivals that focused on the agricultural cycle throughout the year. Each festival frequently involved fire in some variety, marked the beginning of an agricultural practice, and paid tribute to the Gods. Wiccans that found this connection to Celtic traditions to be more intriguing than others often lean more into Celtic Wicca.

ALEXANDRIAN WICCA Founded by Alex and Maxine Sanders, Alexandrian Wicca is more eclectic than other Wiccan practices and focuses on the relationship between the God and the Goddess a little bit more than other traditions do. They meet regularly for full moons, new moons, and the eight sabbats.

COCHRANE CRAFT While not strictly Wicca (in fact, Gardner and Robert Cochrane were former coven mates turned adversaries), Cochrane Craft holds the same roots, ritual structures, and deities. This is likely due to the fact that Doreen Valiente had about as much a hand in guiding Cochrane practices as she did the practices for the Gardnerian traditions. Cochrane Craft is also sometimes referred to as Traditional Witchcraft.

Book of Shadows

A Book of Shadows is a book of spells, ritual methodologies, magical knowledge, mythology, and lore. A coven's Book of Shadows holds the mysteries of their unique lineage and is usually kept safe by the High Priestess. Solo and coven Wiccans alike keep a personal Book of Shadows that hold information pertaining to their areas of interest, research, and magic. Each Book of Shadows is as unique as the Wiccans who own them. For example, one Book of Shadows may be stuffed with crystal magic, specific manifestation spells, and directories of the magical properties of herbs, while others may focus exclusively on developing their relationship with the God and Goddess.

A Book of Shadows is usually handwritten for two reasons: The act of physically writing in a personal book channels magic to an individual's Book of Shadows, and transcribing information serves to better incorporate it into the reader's core knowledge. Adding sketches and other forms of art helps channel more energy into a Book of Shadows.

Modern Types of Wiccans

Witches break the mold, so trying to sort Wiccans into specific tidy categories will never work. However, the descriptions that follow offer a general sense of the different types of practicing Wiccans. Are there other types? Of course! Continue to be the inquisitive witch that you are and seek out a practice that serves you well.

RECONSTRUCTIONIST

Reconstructionist Wiccans attempt to rebuild very specific, ancient, pre-Christian traditions into a modern, neo-pagan practice. They focus on a singular cultural origin (such as Nordic runes, African orishas, or Druidism) and seek to recreate the old magic as much as possible. This can be very difficult for someone who doesn't have the resources to research complex source documents. Reconstructionism was popular at the beginning of Wicca when Margaret Murray and Gerald Gardner were attempting to find ancient practices to argue for the validity of Wicca as a religion, but it is not as in vogue nowadays. Because most traditions were passed down orally through family members, finding valid and comprehensive written guidance for reconstructionist Wicca is near impossible.

ECLECTIC

Eclectic Wiccans research and gather material that interests them and blend it into a unique practice that works for them. It is mostly what this book will focus on. Eclectic Wicca is great for individuals who are hungry to learn, patient, and persistent. It takes time to build a relationship with the God and Goddess, and learning to differentiate the voice of your own intuition from theirs takes practice.

Due to the "do-it-yourself" nature of eclectic Wicca, it can be difficult for these Wiccans to find a structure that works for them. Picking and choosing from different pagan traditions to carve out a comprehensive practice can make a solo practitioner feel isolated from their religion and the older tradition. Some eclectic Wiccans supplement their own practices by joining covens in their outer courts, which provides some structure while still allowing the freedom to practice as they wish.

SOLITARY

Solitary practitioners are quite common in witchcraft and Wicca. Due to the initiatory nature of Wicca, there was a time when the demand of coven seekers outweighed the number of covens available. At that time, books provided a wealth of knowledge that Wiccans in isolation used to self-teach through trial and error. This type of Wicca offers a great degree of independence. These Wiccans have more agency, and being a motivated self-starter can be invaluable when trying to encourage yourself to pour over source texts that are written to be intentionally enigmatic. Solitary Wiccans will have to seek out masters for guidance if the books prove to be a bit too cumbersome.

I like to think of covens as firehoses and solitary witches as garden hoses, and both have power in their own right. Spells that are specifically tailored to your desires and needs are best performed by you. Covens often work BIG magic, but that magic is often shared by the whole group. Solitary Wiccans can often create enough magic for themselves.

COVEN

Every coven functions differently. Covens gather regularly, but what "regularly" looks like differs from coven to coven. It could be for every esabat (once a month), every sabbat (twice a season), for only the greater or lesser sabbats (once a season), or even weekly.

Coven relationships fall somewhere between an academic cohort, an extremely close group of friends, and a tight-knit found family. Covens keep each other close, and if there is anything short of a strong connection, a better fit may be waiting somewhere in the wings for a witch to find.

Covens often work big magic and share it with the whole group. They foster accountability and help improve personal dedications, but they can also feel stifling to some of the freer spirits. Being intimate with a group of people can also be intimidating if a Wiccan isn't fully settled in themselves or their craft.

Note: Always be safe when meeting strangers and seeking out covens. Meet in public places at first, avoid any up-front conversation of paying to enter a coven, and always tell a trusted friend where you're going and who you're meeting.

Initiation

As a mystery religion, lineaged covens only impart their secrets to initiated members that go through a rite of passage that allows them to enter into the community. Initiation into a coven takes an extended period of time getting to know the history and lore of that coven as well as the members of the coven themselves. Members seeking initiation will often spend time in the Outer Courts of a coven. Traditionally, after a year and a day, an individual may be granted the ability to initiate into a coven if the High Priestess deems it to be a good fit for all parties.

HIERARCHICAL COVENS

Hierarchical covens have degree systems that initiates work their way up through participation in a coven, study, and dedication. Seekers (people who are trying to get initiated into a coven) can participate in Outer Court activities to get to know the coven better. Once initiated, they study under the wisdom of the High Priestess (HPS) and/or High Priest (HP) in a mentor/student relationship. The top of the coven hierarchy take responsibilities of coordinating coven meetings, organizing rituals, and generally leading their coven.

Solo practitioners can self-initiate or self-dedicate through a personal ritual of spiritual rebirth and cleansing (see page 88). After self-initiation, a solo Wiccan can explore the mysteries through thoughtful self-guided research, meditation, and experimentation. Self-initiation, however, does not grant blanket access to a closed community, and practicing in the Outer Courts for a year and a day does not grant initiation to everyone.

NONHIERARCHICAL COVEN

The structure for nonhierarchical covens is more loosely molded and chosen by the coven members. Thirteen witches is the traditional number for a coven, but three could be an excellent way to channel the magic of the rule of three. For covens in this style, coven mates often have a diverse set of skills and rely on the wisdom of each witch's area of interest. For example, one person might specialize in home spirits and kitchen witchery while another might be better at road openers and luck magic.

Monotheism, Ditheism, and Polytheism

While no core belief system is tied to the practice of Wicca, you could be an atheist, of the Abrahamic religions, Taoist, or any other overarching belief system and still practice Wicca. Because Wicca is a religion that worships deities, defining the different types of deity worship will help give a name to the way your craft expresses itself.

MONOTHEISM is the belief that there is only one God. This could be interpreted as the belief that there are *no* other gods, but through the lens of Wicca, this typically means that all Gods are one. They weave together the fabric of the universe in the same way that many pieces of thread create one single piece of cloth.

DITHEISM is what Wicca is most often associated with, because of the two prime deities of the craft: the Triple Goddess and the Horned God. These two beacons have a pull that balance each other and, as such, light up different parts of us. They encourage us to experience dichotomies with a "yes, and" mentality rather than an "either or."

POLYTHEISM is the belief in many Gods. In polytheism, the Gods are usually less all-powerful, and more representative of certain struggles and strengths. Wiccans are polytheist when they explore certain roots and mysteries of the God and Goddess. Paying tribute to representations (as the Maiden, Mother, and Crone, or as different deities from different pantheons, like Apollo and Pan) are ways that Wiccans practice polytheism.

Like much of eclectic Wicca, choose whichever path and belief system sings to you. As long as you practice, there's no right or wrong way to be a Wiccan.

Wiccan Laws

Hold these laws loosely in your palm, like you're sifting through sand to find something sturdy. Calling these "moral guidepost laws" is a bit conflated, considering not every practicing Wiccan adheres to these guidelines, nor do practicing Wiccans of the lineages where the laws originated and were popularized. Many of these laws are intentionally open-ended. The Threefold Law, for example, doesn't prohibit certain practices, but rather informs that whatever you do will come back at you. Three is no Rosetta Stone or base holy text that all Wiccans adhere to. There are Craft Laws, Old Laws, Ardanes, or Ordains that all deviate from each other in different ways. Practicing witchcraft, deep introspection, and a continued desire to learn more about the world around you will help you build your own moral code. Consider these laws to be guidelines that you can use to inform your actions.

WICCAN REDE

The Wiccan Rede, colloquially known as "Ye harm none, do what ye will," is the north star for many Wiccans' moral compass. As with many types of Eastern esotericism, Eastern beliefs (such as of karma) are reflected in the Wiccan Rede. Longer snippets of the Wiccan Rede are often taken from Gwen Thompson's poem "Rede of the Wiccan," and while the language may seem baroque and weathered by time, it was actually published in 1975 in *Green Egg Magazine*.

Living your life and practicing how you will while doing no harm to others encourages Wiccans to be kind, while respecting their own boundaries and desires. Invoke the Wiccan Rede as a chant to build courage against shame and adversity. It can be an empowering mantra when outside sources tell us that what we want in our heart of hearts is wrong. It can also be used when reflecting on interpersonal relationships, the consequences of your actions, and what harm means.

What's listed below are descriptions of several of the most common laws, as well as references to other law systems to illustrate just how many different guidelines there can be.

THREEFOLD LAW

The Threefold Law works in tandem with the Wiccan Rede. While the Rede directs Wiccans to do no harm, the "Rule of Three," as it's sometimes called, dictates a reason why harming people with magic can be bad. Magic seeks balance and looks to course correct when things move out of harmony. Sending out a negative force can throw off the balance and create ripples that can be felt by the caster. For example, if you're casting a spell that would cause someone to break up with their partner, you might in turn experience a break in familial or friendship connection of thrice the magnitude later down the road.

Harm can be represented by removing another person's free will as well as other physical, mental, and emotional stressors. A negative force can be a stroke of bad luck manifesting in tiny inconveniences or an earth-shaking personal catastrophe.

Inferring that bad things are happening to you because you must have done something terrible in your casting is not the goal of the Threefold Law. The Threefold Law and the Wiccan Rede are both moral tools to help Wiccans empathize with the experiences of others and how their will can powerfully manifest.

OTHER WICCAN CODES

There are many other definitions of the ambitions, virtues, and integrities of a witch. None of these are mandatory. They're only here to help you build your own code of conduct.

One of the most prolific codes that has been adhered to and modified for decades is Eliphas Levi's *Four Paws of the Sphinx* (or *Four Powers of the Magus*). Levi was a member of the Hermetic Order of the Golden Dawn. These virtues in transcendental magic were (according to Levi) the powers that guided the magical wisdom of the sphinx. These Four Paws/Powers are:

- To Know
- To Dare
- To Will
- To Keep Silent

Aleister Crowley (a famous occultist and the founder of Thelema) adopted, slightly revised, and renamed these principles, dubbing them the **Witch's Pyramid**.

- To Know
- To Dare
- To Will
- To Keep Silent
- To Go

Additionally, Doreen Valiente's poem, "Charge of the Goddess," has been adopted by many Wiccans over the years. The eight virtues described highlight attributes of the God and Goddess that Wiccans hold in their heart to guide their actions and magic. The **Charge of the Goddess** is:

- Beauty and Strength
- Power and Compassion
- Honor and Humility
- Mirth and Reverence

Crafting your own set of guidelines around the information given here can be an excellent way to connect to the Divine and your practice. Write down your own set of laws that align with your moral code, personal values, and teachings of Wicca in your Book of Shadows.

For more inspiration, seek out Lady Sheba's 161 Rules for the Witch, the 30 Laws of Alexandrian Wicca, or any other moral code tied to a branch of Wicca you're curious about.

Ceremonies

Wicca is a ritualistic practice, and as such, there are certain times throughout the month and year that hold a more powerful significance to a practicing Wiccan. Honoring these ceremonies is by no means mandatory, and skipping one of these holy days will not bring bad luck or anything of that sort into the fold. View these special days as opportunities to reaffirm your connection to yourself and the God and Goddess.

ESABATS

Esabats are moon-focused celebrations aligned with the sacred feminine. They are traditionally honored with a coven once a month on the full or new moon (depending on the types of rituals performed) and are directly tied to the Goddess. A year holds thirteen esabats, which usually corresponds to the number of members in covens. The different phases of the moon throughout its cycle represent the different forms of the Triple Goddess: The new moon is the Maiden (visually represented by a crescent moon), the full moon is the Mother, and the waning moon is the Crone (visually represented by a half moon). The moon's twenty-eight-day cycle follows the natural menstrual cycle of those assigned female at birth. If you've ever heard about Wiccans' reputation for dancing naked under the full moon, the esabat is when they would have stripped bare and howled at their holy Lady.

While skyclad rituals are still practiced in some covens, the frequency of the esabat usually lends itself to a calmer affair. Some Wiccans feel pressured to pay reverence to the Goddess for each esabat, but the Goddess does not demand the constant validation. If you do feel compelled to honor her for every turn of the moon but struggle to make space for a weekly ritual, simply saying a few words in her honor or lighting a single candle is an excellent way to practice Wicca without pressure.

Esabats are when Wiccans put in the regular work for magic. Additionally, every full moon carries its own power and means something different to the Goddess. See page 42 for specific notes on how to time your spells to the phases of the moon.

⌾— SABBATS —⌾

Sabbats are the masculine mirror of esabats. They occur much less regularly than esabats and focus more on the sun and fire. Each sabbat tells part of the story of the God and the Goddess and the role they play in the life and death of the sun throughout the year. Each festival is a time for gathering and paying tribute to the God and Goddess, and it marks a shift in energy in the natural cycle of the seasons. Sabbats include four lesser sabbats centered on solar holidays and four greater sabbats corresponding to the earth festivals of the cross-quarter days.

There are two primary cultural sources of sabbats: Celtic and Germanic pre-Christian traditions. Germanic traditions follow the four solar holidays (placed on equinoxes and solstices) and are the lesser sabbats. Celtic traditions focus on the four cross-quarter days nestled directly between an equinox and a solstice.

If esabats are when Wiccans put in the work, then sabbats are when that work is celebrated. There are no specific rules about celebrating all pagan holidays. Some traditions celebrate only the lesser sabbats, while others celebrate only the greater sabbats. Others celebrate all eight.

Skyclad

Skyclad means "wearing only the sky," or "nude" for the uninitiated. Wiccans will often strip off their garments to better break free from what is normal and expected. Ritual nudity is never regarded judgmentally, but rather like a tool to help channel your mind into a space to practice. It also encourages us to slip more fully into our skins and love this vessel that we live in. Performing a ritual skyclad may be jarring at first, but breaking from the norm and changing mindsets is kind of the point. Working skyclad is completely optional and a personal choice for all Wiccans, and can be done or forgone for any reason.

⸙ LESSER SABBATS ⸙

The four lesser sabbats correspond to the different solstices and equinoxes that follow the change in Gregorian seasons (autumn, winter, spring, and summer) on solstices and equinoxes. Solstices are the longest and shortest days of the year and correspond with when the sun reaches either its highest or lowest point in the sky for the year. Equinoxes occur directly between the solstices and are when most places on the planet experience roughly the same amount of night as they do day.

The lesser sabbats correspond to Anglo-Saxon and Germanic pre-Christian festivals. The vernal equinox is celebrated with Ostara, the midsummer solstice is celebrated with Litha, the autumnal equinox is celebrated with Mabon, and the winter solstice is celebrated with Yule.

The four greater sabbats are nestled between each equinox and solstice. Also known as earth festivals or cross-quarter days, the greater sabbats tie into ancient Gaelic and Celtic agricultural calendars. The different celebrations correspond with the seasons as we know them: winter for Samhain, spring for Imbolc, summer for Beltane, and Lughnasadh for autumn. Each of these festivals is based on an ancient Celtic fire festival, and you can see the imagery bleed through in their traditional rituals.

The lesser sabbats acknowledge peak moments in the earth's, moon's, and sun's astrological journey, while the greater sabbats are usually when everything we love about a season is at its peak.

The Divine and the Wheel of the Year

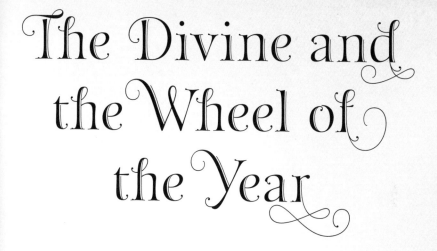

They go by many names, and one of the great mysteries for you to uncover will be learning what name they answer to for you. Their cosmic dance mimics the season's cycle in a year and the give and take of life and death. Dredge the texts and dive in deep to the mythology of the Divine.

Wiccan Deities

Wicca's primary deities are the God and Goddess, divine masculine and feminine. They can be seen through different lenses in different cultural heritages, and some traditions only call them Lord and Lady. They answer to many names (Cernunnos and Aradia, Woden and Freya, Dagda and the Morrigan), and the lore behind each of their sacred names is often unique and accompanied by specific ritual practices and symbols. Their names may change from year to year, sabbat to sabbat, or with the phases of the moon. When seeking out their visages for yourself, try to keep the pairings distinct, that is, do not pick the name of a Greek Goddess and a Celtic God when calling them down.

Their influence frequently manifests as a call or a deep desire to indulge in something potentially a little out of character for you. If an aspect of Diana is trying to reach out, archery may become deeply more interesting than it was before. If pyrography becomes irresistible, perhaps the god of fire seeks to ignite your creativity. As always, ensure your safety whenever connecting to the God and Goddess in new ways. Your health and safety are their prime concern, and they wouldn't want you to risk it in their honor.

It is completely normal to be called to one deity more than the other if a more powerful masculine or feminine energy calls to you at certain times in your life. As you research more about their histories, gifts, and domains, you'll grow closer and closer to the Divine. Continue to seek out texts to expand your knowledge of the God and Goddess in their many forms to deepen your connection.

GREAT GODDESS

The Great Goddess is our most holy moon and earth mother. Her receptive energy cradles life as we know it on earth. She rules over the earth and moon and her power turns the tides of the sea. The splendor of her beauty is all around us when we experience nature and all its wild and feral gifts. She is free and loves all of those in her care. She is the feminine aspects of ourselves that we nurture and grow with tender attention. She is the moon in the sky and the earth beneath our feet. She is the expansive cosmos, the void of space, and the bright and glorious earth.

Wiccan representations of her frequently show her as the Triple Goddess: Maiden, Mother, Crone. While this representation is primarily of the phases of the moon (waxing, full, and waning), the Triple Goddess is also reflected in her domain of the earth. Her name can be that of moon goddesses, fertility goddesses, goddesses of the fire and hearth, or goddesses of love and

beauty. Research different Wiccan pantheons to help deepen your connection to the many different forms of the radiant Goddess. Point your palms toward the earth to receive her energy or reach your arms up toward the sky in a wide-legged stance to channel her in Goddess pose.

When a likeness is needed for her, but an appropriate statuette is unattainable, the Goddess can be represented by a cauldron, cup, mirror, or shell. She adores flowers, specifically five-petaled flowers or flowers that only open for the moon. Adorn yourself and her likeness with silver, pearls, and emeralds. All of the earth's creatures are her children, but the rabbit, owl, hounds, bees, and cats are particularly sacred to her. She sits at the seat of intuition and offers her wisdom to those who care to listen.

Work with the Goddess by setting goals and spells to the cycles of the moon. She is with you when you tend to your needs and the needs of others. Give her offerings of fresh flowers and bury crystals in the earth under her moonlight. Compost your food scraps to help her in keeping the land rich and fertile. Freewrite in the dark moon to get to know the wisdom of your shadow self with her help.

∾ TRIPLE GODDESS ∾

The Triple Goddess is frequently tied to the Greek goddess of witchcraft, Hecate (or Hekate). Although she has claimed the name now, it was not originally part of lore and the Triple Goddess's three roles were more aligned to the three Fates.

Many world religions and mythologies have representations of the Triple Goddess. The Triple Goddess symbolizes three of the main aspects of the Goddess: abundant possibilities, loving-kindness and fertility, and wisdom. Sometimes it is three separate goddesses that are tied intricately together, or a single goddess who, over the course of her mythological lifetime, embodies all three aspects of the Triple Goddess.

Maiden

As the Maiden, the Goddess sees the world brightly with the dewy-eyed radiance of youth. She is a seed, budding with potential, and the first rain of spring that nourishes the parched earth. She is the whisper of distant possibilities and the gentle nudge to start the wheel in motion. The Maiden offers a promise of good things to come. Her love is as free and warm as the light she radiates. She can symbolize innocence and purity in the sense that the weight of the world and its wisdom doesn't yet weigh heavy on her brow.

As mentioned on page 44, when in her Maiden form, she is the waxing moon and is specifically represented as the waxing crescent in the Triple Goddess symbol.

Mother

The Mother is a symbol of abundance and the many wonderful offerings of our home, the earth. She is a warm summer breeze and the bounty of the first harvest. She's the excitement of a plan beginning to fall into place and the deep drive that helps you follow through. She is a love unblinking, an open heart of forgiveness, and an intimate understanding of what it means to be alive.

As mentioned on page 46, when in her Mother form, she is the full moon and resides as a full circle or pentagram at the center of the Triple Goddess symbol.

Crone

The Crone sits quietly in the corner, weaving her fate and observing all. She is at once the bony hand of death gripping your heart with grief and the tender hope of rebirth and new beginnings that come with endings. She is associated with many of the witch Goddesses in mythology (the Morrigan, Hecate, and Baba Yaga). Some may fear the sharp knife of her wisdom and what it means to face your own mortality, but the Crone offers her guidance and wisdom to those who are open to receiving it.

The moon is waning when the Crone reigns, and while she can be aligned with a loss of strength, there is power in the dark and mysteries are easier to uncover under her moon. The Crone is represented as the waning crescent on the right of the pentagram of the Triple Goddess symbol.

Jungian Archetypes

The God and Goddess are sometimes said to be Jungian archetypes, or similar entities of a collective consciousness. There are sun, moon, and fertility gods in many different cultures, and Carl Jung postulated that this was due to universal human experiences and patterns. You'll often hear in Wicca and witchcraft to "take what serves you and leave what doesn't." It's a solid motto for practices and beliefs, but it can be a bit colonial and appropriative when done without care. Jungian archetypes expand upon this idea. Because there are many sun Gods and fertility Goddesses, we can see Wiccan divine in the roots of many different pantheons. The names of the God and Goddess may come to you, or you can seek out where their roots overlap with your own.

HORNED GOD

In the past, the horns have given the impression that the Horned God is the same as the Christian devil, Satan, but that is not the case. The Horned God is the sun embodied and the source of life. He is the divine masculine, and he projects strength and the pleasant warmth of the sun among all who love him (and those who don't). He feeds the fields so that we may partake in his bounty, and he cycles through the Wheel of the Year as the world blooms and dies. He is the tender heart of wild animals as well as the god of the hunt. He is the intimate relationship between predator and prey.

He is barefoot in the woods and a driving force of ambition walking alongside you as you snatch your dreams. There is wheat in his beard and flowers in his hair that shimmer with the glare of his gold knife. As the Wheel of the Year turns, the mythology of the God follows the astrological movements of the sun and embodies the warm and life-giving nature of it. He is a god of sex, passion, and love and he is as fearsome or as gentle as you choose to see him.

Work with the Horned God by offering milk, wine, and honey at your shrines to the earth. Singing, chanting, and dancing will draw him close. Showing love to plants and tamed animals and being respectful for all wild things will honor him. He appears in many different forms, but his symbols include horns, spears, swords, wands, arrows, and sometimes a phoenix. Open your palms up to project his energy.

Answering to many names and taking many forms, he is most commonly called Lord, Witch King, or the Great Horned God. You may also seek him out as Pan, the Leader of the Wild Hunt, Lord of Death, Cernunnos, Lugh, the Green Man, Osiris, Ra, or Apollo.

HOLLY KING AND OAK KING

Every year, the earth has two kings. The Oak King of the light rules from the winter to the summer solstice and the Holly King of the dark rules from the end of Litha to Yule. Every solstice the two do battle: light and dark dancing more than trying to actually win. Some tales say they are different aspects of the same God, and others say that they are brothers of light and dark.

Cycles of the Moon

Every month or so, our mother moon waxes and wanes
through cycles as an ever-present reminder that growth,
change, and culling are natural parts of a cycle that is constantly
in motion. Each phase of the moon charges the dark earth with
a unique type of energy that witches can amplify and direct with
each pass. Waxing moons are a great time to cast spells that add
something to your life and waning moons are an excellent time
to try and remove things that are no longer serving you. When
performing spells that require several days of dedication, try to
cast at the same time each day. Not only will that time be more
charged, but it will also help ensure that you don't miss a day.

Many Wiccans practice jarring moon water (see page 141) or
setting out a jar of water to be blessed by the powers of the moon.
This can be used in rituals and spells, or just to water your plants
to bring a simple garden blessing.

What follows is a detailed list of the energies active during the cycles of the moon. This information is meant to guide, but not to be prohibitive. Casting a manifestation spell during the waning moon will not have negative effects if other elements are aligned and there is a need. However, if something feels off, you could try flipping your spell. For example, if you'd like to draw something to you during a waning phase, consider how you could reframe it as banishing an alternate energy. There is balance in everything, and you have the power to break tired ways of thinking and make the magic happen.

⧸⧹ — NEW MOON — ⧹⧸

The new dark moon is a liminal space between the end and beginning of every lunar month. Wiccan esabats are usually celebrated on the full moon in the cycle, but celebrating the dark moon as an esabat is also a common practice. It is entirely dependent on the energy that the individual or group wants to work with for that esabat.

Astronomically speaking, new moons are when the moon is aligned between the earth and the sun. So, while we cannot see our lovely lady moon, know that at this time the God and Goddess in all of her forms are close and consorting.

Because it is the cusp between the beginning and the end, individuals may feel sluggish or prone to a dip in mood and negative thoughts during this phase. Endings are a good time to take a breath and rest. Release anything you've been holding on to that no longer serves you. This moon is also a great time for any final acts of banishment magic.

The Goddess is on the cusp of the Crone and Maiden during this phase of the moon, and it lasts one day. Magic tied to this moon is best performed at sunrise, the moment when the night meets the day and the darkness finds the dawn.

ᚥ— WAXING CRESCENT —ᚥ

As the Goddess grows in power, so does light begin to stretch across the moon. The Goddess is in her Maiden phase during this moon, and she encourages us to tackle things with a childlike wonder we may have thrown off with our youth. Use this time to shamelessly pursue new passions or rediscover old ones. Ask questions and be insatiably curious. The energy in this moon can be a little frantic with the wealth of possibilities and paths that may be open to you. Using road openers or divination tools to help you choose the path you'd like to pursue is an excellent way to harness the boundless joy of a Maiden Goddess.

It's a great time to have wild daydreams and let your mind run away with rampant possibilities. Set new goals and observe all you have with wild wonder. Waxing crescents are also good times to consider road-opener spells, perform ritual purifications, and cleanse yourself and your tools. This phase lasts for six or seven days. Start spells that are meant to attract at the beginning of this cycle and perform them at the same time every night during the waxing phase of the moon to build their power.

FIRST QUARTER MOON

First quarter moons are a great time to
check in with yourself and any spells that
you're performing over an extended
period. Check in with your initial
intentions. Take stock in the bounties
you have and relentlessly express
gratitude for even the smallest things.
Acknowledging the good you have will bring
more of the same kind of excellence to your life.

The Goddess is in her Maiden phase during this moon and the
phase lasts one day. Spells tied to this moon are best performed
at noon.

WAXING GIBBOUS

Still young and growing, the waxing
gibbous has all of the energy of youth.
The Maiden calls to be directed toward
a project, spell, or area where growth
is desired. Spells meant to draw things
toward you are potent in this section of
the waxing moon. This is an excellent time
to go all out. During this phase as the waxing
moon fills up the cup to full, full moon themes of abundance
can be celebrated. Allow your effort to pour out of you and throw
your whole heart into whatever practices and magic you're
working on. Solidifying strong bonds and partnerships
during the waxing gibbous sets the relationship up to be
celebrated in the coming full moon.

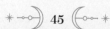

The Goddess is in her Maiden phase during this moon and transitioning into the Mother. A waxing moon that falls on a Thursday is a good time to complete a spell you've been working on for some time. This phase lasts six or seven days.

⌁— FULL MOON —⌁

Full moons often coincide with a high level of chaotic energy. As the full moon pulls the tides, so too does it manipulate the energy in our bodies. This can manifest in the clearing of a particularly ambitious to-do list, making rash or passionate decisions, or feeling heightened levels of anxiety. Count your blessings and acknowledge your accomplishments when the moon is full. All prayers and pleas to her have a higher chance of being heard and responded to.

Rituals performed on this day should invoke the Drawing Down the Moon ritual (see page 137) to bring the Goddess to the table and fully incorporate her power. If you feel called to recreate any of the many images and depictions of witches dancing around a bonfire, do so and raise energy to the full moon above. Simple ways to harvest the magical energy of this full moon is to take time to bask in the bright moonlight. Any spells to encourage growth, manifestation, or draw things to you should be completed on the full moon.

The Goddess is in her Mother phase. Spells tied to this moon are at their highest power at sunset. This phase lasts one day, and the Goddess is at the peak of her power.

WANING GIBBOUS

Waning and loss can often have negative connotations, but it is not in nature's nature to grow without pause. This is a slow release from an abundance attitude filled with bustling energy to the humble quiet of a night alone at home. The waning gibbous is the beginning of the end, a dimming to dark. This process is meant to balance the energy building that occurs during the waxing moon.

The waning moon is also a time to rest and assess how best to finish off the cycle strong. It is common to feel depleted as the moon begins to hide, especially after the revelry of a full moon. Use the waning gibbous as a cue to pause and reflect.

Spells for removal of obstacles, banishment of bad vibes, and pruning of broken bits will be empowered here. For stronger castings, start spells on the first night of the waning gibbous moon and finish them on the new moon.

The Goddess is in her Mother phase during this moon, though she is transiting into her Crone phase. This phase lasts six or seven days.

THIRD QUARTER MOON

The Goddess glances back and we see her partially as she leaves us. This half-moon is for reflection. Look upon your acts of the past lunar month and see how your actions align with the compass of your soul. Ask yourself how you can finish off the ethos of this lunar month strongly. As with the waxing first quarter moon, take time to express and experience gratitude for what you have done.

The Goddess is in her Crone phase. This phase lasts one day. Spells tied to this moon are best performed at midnight.

WANING CRESCENT

The end of this cycle is nigh, and the waxing crescent acts as the harbinger of a fresh start. The Crone remembers where you've started and holds all the lessons that you've learned. Embrace her wisdom and the knowledge that nothing is certain and only fools are positive. Inspect any questions or poke around at  the corners of mysteries with an insightful eye, but avoid chasing them with the lust of the Maiden. This is a time for earned rest, and you deserve it.

During this phase, themes of finality, completion, and expulsion are all prevalent. Embrace the release of old habits. Pull yourself out of the rabbit hole you fell down earlier in the cycle and take a deep, clean breath of fresh air. Allow this moon to pull tears and regrets from you and, rather than fighting their existence, acknowledge them for the lessons they've taught you. Be especially kind to yourself during this phase and the phase that follows. Sometimes it's hard to embrace the darkness and look our shadows in the face.

The Goddess is in her Crone phase and transitioning into the Maiden. This phase lasts six or seven days.

Many Magnificent Moons

The Old Farmer's Almanac marks each month's moon with a popular colloquial name (frequently appropriated from non-connected Native American cultures). Many Wiccans research the different names for the full moons locally, from their heritage, or ascribe them their own meaning as they notice annual personal patterns. For example, if you consistently get into relationships in the month of July, perhaps you rename July's moon the Lover's Moon. Perhaps you do most of your ancestor work in March to celebrate a birthday of the beloved dead. In that case, the Dead Moon would make sense for you.

I've followed the Old Farmer's Almanac moons on the following pages and provided common medieval English (if different from the Almanac) and neo-pagan names as well (some of which are the same). As you begin to celebrate the esabats more, keep a record of the energy you want to channel in each of these months. Research moon lore relevant to where you live or celebrate every moon with a practiced routine.

MONTH	MOON NAME	DESCRIPTION
January	Wolf Moon / Ice Moon	Named for the howling of wolves. Early Europeans in America thought that wolves howled when they were hungry, but we know now that wolves howl to claim territory and locate family. The Wolf Moon is a time to replenish your boundaries, fill up your cup, and seek comfort or warmth from your dearest companions.
February	Hungry Moon / Storm Moon / Snow Moon	The Hungry Moon comes after a period of rest and hibernation and symbolizes the beginning of the end of the season of rest. This moon is used as a time of reflection to help chart a course forward.
March	Worm Moon / Chaste Moon/ Dead Moon	The Worm Moon is a moon of emergence. It specifically references a type of beetle larva in South Dakota that emerges from tree bark as winter thaws. This esabat is for laying the gritty groundwork for a strong start. It encourages us to shake off the sleepy shrug of winter and reemerge into the world.
April	Pink Moon / Seed Moon / Awakening Moon	The Pink Moon is named for the phlox (also known as pink moss) and other flowers that start to emerge. The energy of this moon is still a strong starting energy, but it's a bit softer. It's for reminding ourselves of little victories and why the work is worth it. Use the Pink Moon as a moment to express gratitude, pat yourself on the back, and give yourself reasons to keep going.
May	Flower Moon / Hare Moon / Grass Moon	Named for the flowering season of North America, the Flower Moon is also sometimes called the Budding or Planting Moon in Native American cultures. The Flower Moon is a moon of hope and potential. Warmer weather is on the horizon, and it is also a signal to start planting seeds for your next season's harvest (whether that harvest is metaphorical or physical).
June	Strawberry Moon / Dyan Moon / Planting Moon	June's moon has many other names as well: Honey Moon, Mead Moon, Egg-Laying Moon, and Hatching Moon. This moon calls forward ripening potential. When honoring this moon, build excitement for the small happy harvest of spring efforts. Indulge in the seemingly childish things that keep you young and nurture your inner youth to keep this moon happy.

MONTH	MOON NAME	DESCRIPTION
July	Full Buck Moon / Mead Moon / Rose Moon	While esabats are tied to the Goddess, the Full Buck Moon is an excellent time to tie the Horned God into your esabat rituals. This moon is named for when a buck's antlers grow the most. Bucks shed their antlers once a year and grow larger sets as they age. This moon encourages us to celebrate how we grow and the cyclical nature of growth.
August	Sturgeon Moon / Corn Moon / Lightning Moon	The Sturgeon Moon is named after an aquatic "living fossil." Sturgeons are a catfish-like fish that stir up waterbeds to find suitable food. This moon is about seeking out and seizing what lights your heart, whether you're the sturgeon sifting through the silt on the river floor or the fisherman hoping that the right opportunity bites.
September	Harvest Moon / Barley Moon	The Harvest Moon occurs closest to the fall equinox and is habitually quite punctual in the way it rises and falls. On occasions when the fall equinox happens in other months, September's moon can also be called the Corn Moon. This moon is for reaping what you've sown, whether it's a plentiful harvest or a sparse one. It's also time for expressing gratitude to others and ourselves for our hard work.
October	Hunter's Moon / Blood Moon	The Hunter's Moon is always the moon that follows directly after the Harvest Moon, which means that it could occur either in October or November. The Hunter's Moon was a signal to prepare for winter, to gather all that we need before a long cold rest settled into our bones. It can also be called the Blood Moon to symbolize the by-product of the hunt or the colors of the leaves as the seasons change.
November	Beaver Moon / Snow Moon / Tree Moon	The Beaver Moon notices how all of the animals in the natural world begin to batten down the hatches in preparation for a bitter freeze. Use this moon to prepare the home and hearth for the extra use they experience in the upcoming season.
December	Cold Moon / Oak Moon / Long Night Moon	Like the solstice, this moon is meant to be a reminder of hope. It can be easy to get lost in the dark when night stretches on and the sun hides away. The Cold Moon is meant to remind us that light will return and that seasons pass. This moon extends its light after it sets for the longest out of all of the moons to help guide our paths.

Wheel of the Year

The Wheel of the Year is the basis of many Wiccan rituals. It follows the life and death of the sun and focuses on the nuanced difference between night and day. In this cosmic dance, the God and the Goddess complement and support each other as the sun and earth. During this time, the God is born, grows to his full power, nourishes the land, and dies. Likewise, the Goddess moves through her cycle of Maiden, Mother, and Crone as the earth bursts with fertility and then gently goes to sleep. The two deities support each other, and if the God's symbol is fire, the Goddess is the torchbearer that helps us wield it.

The different celebrations in the Wheel of the Year are rooted deeply in Celtic traditions but you can see the influence of traditions from other European roots for the different ceremonies. Based on the Celtic calendar, solstice and equinox celebrations are known as quarter days, with cross-quarter days nestled

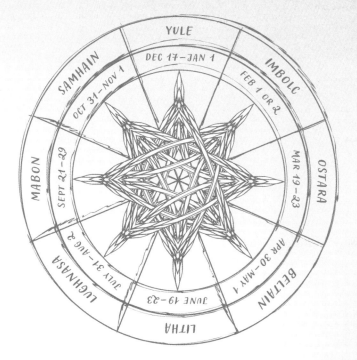

snuggly between the two. Cross-quarter days are the greater
sabbats and when the seasons begin in earnest.

Quarter days and cross-quarter days are important to all
natural religions, seeing as they're rooted in the changing of
the seasons. These days were important for celebration and
communion with the land, and they marked beginnings and
ends to cyclical practices. Additionally, there are many Christian
celebrations that follow these holy Wiccan holidays (Easter on
Ostara, Christmas on Yule, and Candlemas for the purification of
the Virgin Mary on Imbolc). These days hold power and meaning,
and honoring yourself and the world we live in are the ways we
show appreciation for the blessings of the God and Goddess.

The Wheel of the Year starts on the greater sabbat of Samhain
or the lesser sabbat of Yule, depending on whether you prefer to
start with the death or rebirth of the God.

YULE

Northern Hemisphere: December 17–January 1

Southern Hemisphere: June 17–July 1

Other Names: Feast of Saturnalia, Julbot, Christmas, Krampus Festival

Type: Winter solstice, lesser sabbat

Goddess Representation: Crone going to sleep until spring

God Representation: God is birthed

Symbols: Yule log, garlands, small potted tree, wreath, Wheel of the Year

Plant Allies: Evergreens (pine, rosemary, bay, juniper, cedar), holly, mistletoe, ivy

Scents: Cinnamon, citrus, ginger, cloves

Foods: Fruits (apple, orange, pears), nuts, pork, warm beverages (cider, wassail, hibiscus and ginger tea)

Colors: Red, white, green

ORIGINS AND HISTORY

Depending on how you look at the calendar, Yule or Samhain is the beginning of the Wiccan calendar. Some people prefer to start on Samhain because it's considered the Wiccan New Year, while others shy away from starting the year with death, which is why many start the Wheel of the Year with Yule and the birth of the God.

In the Wiccan mythology of Yule, God has been reborn from the Goddess and she's slumbering to recover until spring. The God is an infant, which is why the days are short, the Goddess is slumbering, and the earth is cold and sleeping with her.

The winter solstice is the shortest day of the year. It is both a beginning and an end and symbolizes annual rebirth. It is a reminder to keep hope in the darkest of times because just as the sun will return, things will also get better.

Much of the imagery of Yule may already be familiar to you. Gathering together to wait out the darkest time of the year fosters a sense of community. Giving gifts is a symbol of gratitude and deep belief that while things may be sparse while the earth slumbers, abundance will come again, and it's meant to be shared. Twelve days of light and celebration is common across many pre-Christian European traditions. A tradition of oath making during Yule can be seen reflected in New Year's resolutions. Evergreen garlands and citrus fruits adorned with cloves remind us that it is possible to thrive in cold and adversity.

Celebrate this sabbat with warm fires, good company, and a bright-eyed hope.

Energy

~ Rebirth

~ Hope

~ Celebration of the return of the sun

~ Change

~ Fellowship

~ Good fortune

~ Gratitude

~ Liminal spaces

Practices

~ Gift giving

~ Foraging

~ Hunting after harvest

~ Keeping a flame for twelve nights

~ Oath making

~ Toasting

~ Festivities

~ Kitchen witchery

~ Communing with the spirits

ᏈᏬ IMBOLC ᏬᏈ

Northern Hemisphere: February 1 or 2

Southern Hemisphere: August 1 or 2

Other Names: Candlemas, Groundhog Day, Brigid's Day, Imbolg

Type: Cross-quarter day, greater sabbat

Goddess Representation: The Maiden awakening

God Representation: Baby or toddler

Symbols: Lambs, milk, white candles, Brigid crosses, straw boys, besoms, fire

Plant Allies: Rosemary, snowdrops, crocuses, daffodils

Scents: Pine, lavender, peppermint, cinnamon

Foods: Dairy (butter, cheese, milk, yogurt), root vegetables (potatoes and carrots), spicy food (chili and curries), soups (colcannon or wild onion soup)

Colors: White, red, orange, yellow

Ꮘ ORIGINS AND HISTORY Ꮼ

This holiday celebrates a journey out of the dark and into the light of spring. It falls at the halfway point between the winter solstice and the spring equinox in the northern hemisphere. The Goddess is recovering from giving birth to God at Yule. She's making her transition from the Crone and returning to herself as the Maiden.

The roots of this tradition lie in Ireland, Scotland, and the Isle of Man. In the Celtic calendar, Imbolc marks the beginning of lambing season. The holiday's name is derived from the Celtic word for "in the belly," *imbolc*. Newborn lambs brought milk, the hope for a warm spring, and an end of the cold days of winter. The Celtic Goddess (and Catholic saint) Brigid is both a Triple Goddess and a fire deity that reigns over this day. While considered a Goddess, they are often associated with both genders. Saint Brigid (while not the Goddess) accepts offerings of poetry and well-smithed items.

The cross-quarter day has also been repurposed by Christian traditions to Candlemas, or the purification of the Virgin Mary. Groundhog Day has its roots in Gaelic weather folklore as the ancient Celts believed that if Imbolc was sunny, it meant that winter was going to last for six more weeks. Weather divination through tarot cards can help Wiccans set intentions for the weeks between Imbolc and Ostara.

Energy

- Healing recovery
- New beginnings
- Strengthening practices
- Home
- Hearth
- Reconnecting to the earth
- Fertility
- Banishing the winter season
- Self-dedication
- Writing and reading poetry
- Nurturing the new year
- Fire and the thaw

Practices

- Spring cleaning
- Feasting and leaving food and wine for Brigid
- Dianic Wiccan initiations
- Blessing tools in the sun
- Fire scrying
- Meditation on energies to leave buried in winter
- Ritual planting and blessing of seeds
- Lighting every lamp in the house at sunset

OSTARA

Northern Hemisphere: March 19–23

Southern Hemisphere: September 19–23

Other Names: Eostra's Day, Vernal Equinox,
Bacchanalia

Type: Lesser sabbat, vernal equinox

Goddess Representation: Maiden

God Representation: Toddler

Symbols: Seeds, blossoms, bees, caterpillars,
butterflies, eggs, bunnies, ladybugs

Plant Allies: Daffodils, lilacs, honeysuckles,
nasturtiums

Scents: Lavender, vanilla, honey

Foods: Stuffed flowers (squash flowers or nasturtiums),
young greens (sprouts, fiddleheads, ramps), sweets
(carnation cupcakes, lavender or lilac syrup for
cordials), fertility foods (eggs, milk, honey)

Colors: Green, lilac, yellow, other pastels

ORIGINS AND HISTORY

While Imbolc signifies the beginning of spring, Ostara beckons
us to enjoy all its beauty. As an equinox, this holiday deals with
balancing the joys of new life with the grief of death. Likewise,
on this equinox there are equal parts light and dark. As the God
grows and our days stretch, he reaches toward maturity while still
full of youthful innocence and wonder. The Goddess manifests in
all of spring's symbols of awakening. She awakens from her deep
sleep and the whole world wakes with her.

Ostara's name comes from the Germanic Goddess of spring
renewal: Eostre. Eostre symbolizes spring and the dawn and

promises prosperity and growth. Honor her with young plants in fresh water. Plant flowers, herbs, and early spring harvests in her name. There is a Ukrainian tradition of blowing the yolks out of eggs to paint detailed scenes on the delicate shell. Christian Easter has adopted many of the traditions and practices of Ostara, so like Yule, the traditions have been kept alive.

As pollination begins and the flowers bud to bloom, Ostara is a time to set intentions for the warmer months of the year, to make room for all of our hallowed hopes and cleanse out stale or stagnant energies. The earth recreates herself every spring, and you too can exude abundant creativity. Take risks, be bold, and let yourself grow.

Energy

- Youthful innocence
- Rebirth and growth
- Cleaning and cleansing
- Balance and harmony
- Reverence for life
- Experiencing nature
- Setting intentions and making plans
- Harmony and balance

Practices

- Planting seeds and seed magic
- Garden blessing
- Cleansing bath
- Spring foraging
- Earth meditation
- Spring altars with fresh flowers
- Working with local plant allies
- Touching grass and getting to know your weeds

BELTANE

Northern Hemisphere: April 30–May 1

Southern Hemisphere: October 30–November 1

Other Names: May Day, May Eve, Hexennacht, Walpurgis Night, Calan Mai, Floralia

Type: Greater sabbat, cross-quarter day

Goddess Representation: Maiden to Mother

God Representation: God coming of age and in his full power

Symbols: Cauldron filled with flowers, mirrors, maypole, wand, besom, flower crowns

Plant Allies: Summer flowers, vine flowers (morning glory, wisteria)

Scents: Vanilla, fragrant summer flowers

Foods: Baked goods (oat cakes or bannocks, scones, fritters), sweet creams (marigold custard, vanilla ice cream), libations (ale, wine, mead), spicy food (curries, garlic butter)

Colors: White, red

ORIGINS AND HISTORY

Beltane is a twofold holiday. Although I don't highlight many of the named holidays that follow the Wheel of the Year, along with Beltane, I'll also be highlighting Hexennacht because many Wiccans celebrate both for different reasons, and one may sing to you more than the other.

Beltane in Celtic translates to "bright fire," which is appropriate because this is one of the Celtic fire festivals in the Wheel of the Year. In Wiccan lore, Beltane is the holiday when both the God and the Goddess are coming of age. There is a wild and phrenetic

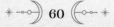

energy to them as they celebrate their youth. This holiday is a celebration of love, fertility, and sex. The maypole is a phallic representation of the God and the flower crown that descends as the maypole is wrapped is symbolic of the Goddess.

The spokes of the Wheel of the Year alternate between Celtic fire festivals and German agricultural festivals. Equally as important as Beltane or May Day is May Eve, also known as Hexennacht. *Hexennacht* in German translates as "witch's night." This also coincides with Walpurgis Night, which celebrates Saint Walpurgis chasing the heathens out of Germany.

While Beltane celebrations involve dancing around the maypole in the bright light of day, Hexennacht celebrations involve dancing around a bonfire cackling late into the night. Both celebrations welcome the energy of spring as the earth soaks up more and more sun.

Energy

- Fertility and reproduction
- Procreation
- Greening of the earth
- Spark of life
- Independence
- Freedom and personal sovereignty
- Manifestation
- Growth as a journey
- Wild abandon
- Love

Practices

- Dancing around the maypole
- Sex magic
- Hedge witchery
- Trance states, traveling, and "flying"
- Ecstatic dance
- Weaving
- Bonfires
- Green witchery
- Communal magic
- Blowing of a horn

⚭ — LITHA — ⚭

Northern Hemisphere: June 19–23

Southern Hemisphere: December 19–23

Other Names: Midsummer, Summer Solstice

Type: Lesser sabbat, summer solstice

Goddess Representation: Pregnant Mother

God Representation: Peak of his strength

Symbols: Mirror toward the sun, fire and flames, the sun, bees, honeycomb

Plant Allies: Sunflower, wisteria, mugwort, St. John's wort, vervain, larkspur, oak, elder

Scents: Chamomile, citrus, sandalwood, lavender

Foods: Alcohol (beer, schnaps, vodka), honey (honey bread, mead), fresh berries (strawberry, blueberry, elderberry), herbs (fresh herbs, leafy green salads, herbed breads)

Colors: White, gold, orange, yellow

⚭ ORIGINS AND HISTORY ⚭

This solar holiday is very much focused on the sun. It is the longest day and the shortest night and when God is at the peak of his power. While Beltane celebrates the union of the God and Goddess, Litha often celebrates the marriage of the God and Goddess. Both God and Goddess have settled into their roles and responsibilities despite the abundant overflow in nature.

Those who follow the mythology of the Oak and Holly King will say that this is when the Oak King (king of light) is at the peak of his power and loses the battle with the Holly King (king of the dark). This symbolizes the sun's dance with the earth as days lengthen and shrink over the course of the year. Litha is the opposite of Yule, which is the shortest day and the longest night, when the Oak King wins the battle against the Holly King as the days begin to lengthen once more.

While Samhain is when the veil to the underworld is the thinnest, Litha is when the veil to the upperworld is the thinnest. Ancient Celts believed that the fairy realm was the thinnest. Spirit work and petitions to the Gods have a high chance of being heard at this time.

The energy this time of year is a lush and fertile world begging to be discovered. Check in with your successes and form new ventures. Explore the natural world around you and forage for plants to preserve and use in winter. Count your blessings and redo your wards at this time when protection magic is most potent.

Energy

- Abundance and ease
- Responsibilities
- Voicing deepest desires
- Gratitude
- Companionship
- Celebrating the day
- Peak power
- Conserving energy
- Divine masculine
- Strength
- Expanding
- Higher powers

Practices

- Intention setting
- Marriages and handfasting
- Outdoor rituals
- Watching the sunrise
- Summer picnic
- Meditating in the sun
- Leaping the bonfire
- Protection magic
- Purification rituals
- Celebration with fire and water
- Pressing flowers
- Manifesting

LUGHNASA

Northern Hemisphere: July 31–August 2

Southern Hemisphere: January 1–February 2

Other Names: Lamas, Loafmass, Lamastide

Type: Cross-quarter day, greater sabbat

Goddess Representation: Pregnant Mother

God Representation: Waning from his peak power

Symbols: Scythe, sun, Triple God, phoenix, corn dolls, wicker and wood baskets

Plant Allies: Poppies, all grains, sunflowers, ginseng, borage, basil, chicory

Scents: Lavender, sage, rose, honeysuckle, sandalwood, frankincense

Foods: Baked goods (breads, pentagram cookies, blackberry pie), corn (cornbread, popcorn, corn on the cob, hominy), fruited beverages (lamaswool, elderflower wine, herbal tea, fruit tisanes, wine, fruited wine), meat cooked over an open fire (barbecued or roasted meats)

Colors: Yellow, red, gold, brown, orange, green

ORIGINS AND HISTORY

Lughnasa (or Lughnasadh) is the last of the Celtic fire festivals in the Wheel of the Year. Named after the Celtic sun God, Lugh, some ancient festivals are said to have lasted a month, or through the Leo season with the astrological calendar. It's the second of the harvest festivals, encouraging the reaping of grains and wheat.

During this time, the Goddess is pregnant. Some traditions honor the Harvest Mother, Mother Earth, or Great Mother at this time when food is a plenty and she is full with child. The warm and gentle guidance of the God can still be felt as the sun continues to support summer's harvest, but the plants of spring are beginning to drop their seeds and the first signs of fall and winter are beginning to show.

This cross-quarter day celebrates hard work and acknowledges death and rebirth in the harvesting and collecting of seeds. Honor this season by taking stock in what you've had, acknowledging where you've been, and charting a course for where you're going. Enjoy nature's bounty and beauty as simple ways to commune with the God and Goddess in their abundant forms. Gather goods for winter and break bread with people you care about. As the sun nourishes the land, we nourish one another.

Energy

- First harvest: grain and wheat
- Reaping what you've sown
- Rewards of labor
- Basking in the energy of nature
- Working on skills and developing craftsmanship
- Survival
- Working contracts
- Conflict resolution
- Acknowledging limits
- Strength in hardship

Practices

- Orchard visits
- Kitchen witchery (specifically baking)
- Blessing seeds
- Seed saving
- Potluck
- Drying herbs
- Wheat weaving
- Prosperity magic
- Bonfires
- Berry picking and harvests
- Manifestation

MABON

Northern Hemisphere: September 21–29

Southern Hemisphere: March 21–29

Other Names: Autumn Equinox, Octoberfest, Witch's Thanksgiving

Type: Lesser sabbat, fall equinox

Goddess Representation: Approaching Crone, wise and wanting to share her experience

God Representation: Near death

Symbols: Spiral, apple, autumn leaves, horn of plenty, cornucopia

Plant Allies: Pine cones, acorns, wheat, dried leaves, pine, ivy, oak branches, milkweed, mums, angelica, butterfly weed, yarrow

Scents: Honeysuckle, sweetgrass, clove, myrrh, black pepper, patchouli

Foods: Canned goods (jams, pickles, fire cider), beans, libations (cider, wine, ale, beer), fruits, seeds

Colors: Red, brown, orange, yellow, purple, violet

ORIGINS AND HISTORY

While labeled Mabon on the Wheel of the Year, some modern Wiccans elect to simply call this holiday the fall or autumnal equinox due to the fact that Mabon is a Welsh fertility God that is not especially tied to this time. Mabon also has loose ties to Arthurian legends, but they're difficult to substantiate.

As with many of the sabbats in the Wheel of the Year, bonfires and ecstatic dance are popular ways to celebrate.

With the height of summer behind us and the days being put to rest, shadow work and grounding rituals are an excellent practice to become comfortable in your own skin and sense of self for the winter.

Energy

- Second harvest: fruits and vegetables
- Balance
- Equality and equilibrium
- Gratitude
- Ephemerality
- Change
- Honesty
- Charity
- Decluttering and clearing
- Optimism
- Blood and found family
- Accountability
- Rest and recovery
- Reaping what you've sown

Practices

- Preparing for winter
- Dedications to learning
- Kitchen witchery
- Elder veneration
- Preservation of food
- Winterizing garden
- Uncovering mysteries
- Besom craft
- Complete projects
- Grounding rituals
- Prosperity
- Shadow work
- Herbalism

SAMHAIN

Northern Hemisphere: October 31–November 1
Southern Hemisphere: April 31–May 1
Other Names: Allhallowtide, All Saints Eve, Day of the
  Dead, Halloween, Midwinter
Type: Cross-quarter day, greater sabbat
Goddess Representation: Pregnant Crone
God Representation: Death of the God
Symbols: Jack-o'-lantern, skulls, candles
Plant Allies: Fallen autumn leaves, marigolds, lilies
Scents: Perfumes and colognes of the beloved dead
Foods: Pomegranates, apples, gourds (butternut
  squash, zucchini, pumpkin), meat (beef, goose,
  lamb), stews, root vegetables (potatoes, carrots,
  turnips)
Colors: Black, red, orange

ORIGINS AND HISTORY

Samhain is the Gaelic name for "summer's end." Many pre-
Christian cultures only celebrated two seasons: summer and
winter. As autumn falls, so does the resplendent abundance of
summer come to a close. In Wiccan mythology, the God of the Sun
has grown old and will pass on during this holiday. The Goddess
is a manifestation of all the wisdom gained in this year and
appears as a pregnant Crone.

Death and endings are deeply emotional occurrences for many
people, but this sabbat is a celebration of the dead. We honor
that everything must pass from this world, even the sun and the
Divine, and that death is a part of life. Samhain is also the third
and final of the harvest festivals, traditionally reaping gourds and

livestock to once again illustrate the connection between life and death on the season's cusp.

At this time, remember that death is not eternal, and for rebirth and new growth to come, some parts must pass on.

Energy

- Witch's New Year
- Third harvest: gourds and animals
- Death and endings
- Shadow self
- Summer's end
- Keeping the light
- Reincarnation
- Divine feminine
- Sacrifice

Practices

- Ancestor veneration
- Divination
- Scrying
- Path working
- Dumb supper
- Lucid dreaming
- Meditation
- Masks
- Working with the thin veil

Five Elements

Ancient alchemists dictated that five elements comprised the fibers of our universe. Their likeness still sings to people today, evidenced by their abundance in fantasy stories in pop culture. Different traditions and lineages invoke the elements in different ways: some have the four physical elements but replace spirit with the Divine, while others align the elements with different directional guardians. In some traditions, the four cardinal guardians are not linked to the elemental spirits at all.

For the purposes of this book, we will adhere to the Common System of elements and directions: north for earth, east for air, south for fire, and west for water. If something about this orientation does not sit well with you, seek out other systems and see whether those traditions suit you better. One other common system is the Northern Quarters System.

Northern Quarters is a Celtic system that acknowledges the four cardinal directions not as elements, but rather as four winds called *airts*. It is used by Cochrane Craft and Celtic Wicca. North corresponds to air, as it is above us. East corresponds to fire, since the sun rises in the east. South is for earth, since it's below our feet. Water is to the west, the location of the West Gate, where the dead travel to the afterlife.

EARTH

Earth is the guardian of the north and the soul of the ground beneath your feet. Our most fertile Mother sleeps here, just under the surface. All of nature's bounty comes from the very earth that grounds and sustains us. Stable and stubborn, the earth is strong and does not bend or break: It endures and can weather the storm of the world above.

When invoking the earth through sound, hear the beat of the drums, the slam of fists on the ground, or the thud of a staff against the earth. To invoke earth without words, hold your hand flat with all of your fingers touching at chest level aligned parallel to the earth.

Earth is the Goddess's domain. It is often represented by either salt or soil on the altar and as a crystal, sand, stones, or the pentacle in Wiccan rituals. Color correspondence is green or brown.

Earth signs of the zodiac are Taurus, Virgo, and Capricorn.

AIR

Guardian of the east and the breath in our lungs, the element of air is fluid and all around us. Air is a mutable element and encourages flexibility and movement. Due to the omniscient nature of air, the element reigns over many of the mental faculties. Psychic power and visualization are ruled by this element, as are the discovery of ancient wisdom and general accumulation of knowledge.

ELEMENTS AND THE PENTACLE

The pentacle is a visual representation of the relationship between the elements. The top of the star represents the spirit (and the Gods) and then north begins at the point clockwise of the spirit (or the point to the right). Some pentacle imagery adds colors to represent the elements and the spirits to the five points.

When representing air through music, wind instruments are played. To invoke the air without words, hold your hand up toward the sky with your fingers splayed wide.

Air is the God's domain. It is often represented by either a bell or incense on the altar and can be represented as a feather, fallen leaves, or wind chimes in Wiccan rituals. Color correspondence is yellow, white, or silver.

Air signs of the zodiac are Gemini, Libra, and Aquarius.

⌒⌒ FIRE ⌒⌒

Guardian of the south, fire burns. Burning away parts of yourself can feel destructive, but controlled burns can be helpful in eliminating harmful habits. Uncontrolled passion can manifest as courage and willpower as much as it can manifest as an explosive anger. Fire encourages us to cull back that which no longer serves us and also symbolizes physical strength and sexuality.

When representing fire through music, string instruments spark an internal flame. To invoke fire without words, hold your hand in a fist, thumb resting against your pointer finger.

Fire is the God's domain. It is often represented by either a red candle on the altar or as chile peppers or cinnamon in Wiccan rituals. Color correspondence is red or orange.

Fire signs of the zodiac are Aries, Leo, and Sagittarius.

WATER

Guardian of the west, the water waits and waves. Ruling rivers, lakes, and the mighty deep of the ocean, it does not trouble itself climbing the mountain. We can feel the energy of the water in ourselves as the undercurrent in our subconscious, a change in the tides toward forgiveness, and a wave of compassion.

Resonant percussive instruments, like cymbals and gongs, emulate the bubbling nature of water. To invoke water without words, hold your hand (or both hands) as a cup.

Water is the Goddess's domain. It is often represented by a bowl of water or chalice on the altar and as a smooth river stone, piece of driftwood, or seashell in Wiccan rituals. Color correspondences are blue or indigo.

Water signs of the zodiac are Cancer, Scorpio, and Pisces.

SPIRITS

The spirit has many names. It is both everywhere and nowhere, within and without, above and below. Known in Sanskrit as Aether and in many Wiccan practices as Akasha, the spirit aligns with no gender or season, and is simply divine in nature. You do not call the spirit, but are rather called by it. Color correspondences are white and black, and it is a symbol of the Wheel of the Year as a whole.

Symbols of Wicca

S ymbols hold power and help channel energy into spells and rituals. This can be symbols woven into clothes, worn on jewelry, carved into candles, or inscribed on written spells. Symbols can represent the power of a certain object or energy. A word of caution: Never use symbols without knowing the full extent of their power. If a symbol calls to you, do your research and seek out its mysteries.

PENTAGRAM Probably the most familiar Wiccan symbol, this five-pointed star in a circle represents the five elements cast in a magic circle. Pentagrams are traditional holy symbols and inscribing it on magical tools or tracing the image during rituals integrates the five elements into the object or practice. Many ritual practices arrange the elemental avatars in the circle to match a pentagram (see page 94).

TRIPLE GODDESS This symbol channels the power of the Goddess in all of her forms: waxing, waning, and full. The symbol is arranged as she appears in the night sky across her cycle: Maiden, Mother, then Crone. Frequently, jewelry or talismans of the Triple Goddess will have a jewel or other object of significance in the center that represents her full moon/Mother aspect.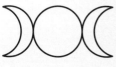

Horned God Also crafted from crescents and circles, the Horned God's symbol channels the divine masculine energy.

Wheel of the Year The wheel turns, and the cycle always continues. This symbol reminds us that nothing is permanent except the passage of time. Each line that splits the circle from its center represents one of the sabbats. It is also the symbol for the spirit.

Solar Cross This is a representation of the sun and the four seasons. This same illustration is also used as the astrological symbol for the earth.

Hecate's Wheel Also known as the Stropholos of Hecate, this symbol was used in Hellenic and Dianic traditions. The Triple Goddess (Maiden, Mother, Crone) is currently deeply associated with Hecate, the goddess of witchcraft. The Stropholos represents Hecate's crossroads domain in its function as a maze. The three similar spirals represent the Triple Goddess's three aspects.

Spiral Goddess This symbol represents the divine feminine power of the Goddess. The image is that of the Mother state, but it is often worked into the Triple Goddess. The spiral at her center also represents the spiral of life and the cyclical nature of the universe. It represents fertility, growth, and new beginnings. It can also be a symbol of hope and opportunity that comes with the sadness and grief of loss.

Seax-Wicca A symbol of Saxon Witchcraft and paganism. The sun and the moon iconography are symbolic of the relationship between the God and the Goddess as well as the dance between the moon, sun, and sabbats.

Celtic Knot/Triquetra The Celtic knot with a Latin name that means "three-cornered" was also claimed by Nordic traditions and found as far west as Germany. It represents the rule of three and connects triads. Whether that's the Triple Goddess, the cycle of life (life, death, rebirth), the order of time (past, present, future), or the orientation of the planes (upperworld, material plane, underworld) is up to interpretation.

Witch's Knot Offers protection from harm and hexes and has general warding properties. It was sometimes used to stave off bad weather. It is also used in binding rituals as a way to protect oneself or loved ones.

Unicursal Hexagram Also representative of Aleister Crowley's religion, Thelema, the hexagram is a type of pentagram. The six points of the star channel different energy than the five points of the pentagram.

Working Wiccan Magic

Ceremonial magic takes time and practice to learn. Tease out these steps piece by piece. Experiment so that you and your witchcraft can learn and grow. Practice regularly and weave small pieces of Wicca into your daily life. Old magic is patient and does not require perfection. Allow yourself to stumble and fall.

Energy Work

Magic is molding different energies with the power of your intention and will to create a desired outcome. Wiccans recognize and channel the flow of the unseen energy of magic. The following terms are key parts of the work that we do, and understanding the nuanced differences in how we work with energy will help you better recognize and feel the changes.

CENTERING Finding your center is focusing on the energy flow in your own body and it brings you back to yourself and gathers energy into your person. A centering practice is the best way to start your rituals. It makes sure that all of the energy in your body is yours and there intentionally. Mindfulness meditations and squared breathing techniques (breathing in to a count of five and out to a count of five) are centering practices.

RAISING Raising energy is traditionally done in the confines of the circle. The circle is there to catch and hold all of the energy raised (usually of a coven) so that it can be channeled by the High Priestess with a specific purpose in mind.

GROUNDING Energy is grounded in one of two ways: energy is returned to the earth after it's been raised in the circle or energy is sent from yourself into the earth as an anchor in times of chaos. The grounding of energy calms and quiets its flow and sends it back to the earth, where it can find roots to feed and bugs to play with.

Visualization is a powerful tool using the theater of the mind. Wiccans use visualization to break down the mundane and imagine better worlds for themselves as well as to evoke unseen energies. It can be done to different degrees and looks different from person to person. One person may be able to clearly see objects in their mind. Others might see their visualizations exclusively in words, or experience an assortment of associations.

As a beginner Wiccan, practice visualizing objects that are familiar to you. Start with a small everyday object. Learn the way it feels in your fingers and the way it looks in direct and indirect light. Then close your eyes and conjure the image in your mind's eye. Take time building it and pay attention to the details you add. Again, this does not have to be a visual recreation in your mind's eye but can instead be a collection of words.

Once you've mastered conjuring small objects in your mind, expand it to larger objects or favorite foods.

Visualizing is a muscle in Wicca that is constantly being exercised and flexed. If it does not come easily for you at the outset, practice and look for different ways visualizations can work for you and your magic.

Once you have the ability to see things in your mind's eye, another part of magic is drawing what you see to you. This is the art of manifestation. Magnetizing certain outcomes or opening certain roads is a form of manifestation. Manifestation is the power of belief made real. Strong visualizations (with lots of specific details) lead to strong manifestations. They work in tandem with the physical actions of an individual to help make the imagined become real.

Wearing lucky charms is a form of manifestation. Goals and to-do lists are a mundane form of manifestation. Petitioning the God and Goddess for assistance is a form of manifestation. On that note, it is important to say that you cannot simply wish something into existence with manifestation. Ambition accompanied by passion will help bring manifestations into reality. The Gods help those who help themselves.

In ritual movement and spellwork, going in a clockwise motion will bring things to you.

Days of the Week

As far as Wiccan magic goes, the days of the week do not hold too much power over the way spells materialize. However, there are subtle differences and correspondences to working spells on certain days.

This guidance should in no way stop you from performing a spell. If you want to perform a protection rite but the evening you have free doesn't meet with energetic alignment of that weekday, shrug it off. Performing the spell is better than putting it off.

- SUNDAY For the sun. Ideal for magic aligned with the God. Cast spells for improved finances, nature's bounty, and protection.
- MONDAY For the moon. Ideal for magic aligned with the Goddess. Cast spells to venerate the ancestors, improve health, or improve memory.
- TUESDAY For Mars. Perform self-dedications on this day. Cast spells for banishment, boundaries, curse or hex breaking, and wards.
- WEDNESDAY For Mercury. An excellent day for business and travel. Cast spells to improve communication, deal with loss, or settle debts.
- THURSDAY For Jupiter. Ideal for magic aligned with the God. Cast spells for honor, oaths, and desires.
- FRIDAY For Venus. Ideal for magic aligned with the Goddess. Cast spells for beauty, love, and pleasure.
- SATURDAY For Saturn. Ideal for magic of the spirit. Cast spells to build personal sovereignty, increase grit, and discover your true self.

Colors

Colors are a tool used to enhance your magic. Choosing certain colors weaves more of your intent, vision, and energy into the magic you cast. This is not an exhaustive list. There is power in making your choice, so research what these colors mean to others and seek out visual alignments that work for you.

- **RED** Fire, passion, courage, impulsivity, love, raw power
- **ORANGE** Sun, protection, attraction, raw power, vitality, ambition, joy
- **BROWN** Animals, earth, decomposition, cycle, strength, common sense, grounding
- **YELLOW** Air, divination, intellect, communication, inspiration, happiness, intuition
- **GREEN** Herbalism, earth, growth, abundance, luck, fertility, renewal
- **BLUE** Healing, water, peace, wisdom, harmony, patience, kindness
- **INDIGO** Psychic awareness, raw emotions, integrity, introspection, adaptability
- **VIOLET** Divine power, spiritual awareness, devotion, peace, optimism
- **WHITE** Purification, meditation, cleansing, full moon, summer, spirit, upperworld, devotion
- **BLACK** Absence, void, night, underworld, honesty, divine energy, greater universe, winter, banishment, protection

Wiccan Tools

The only tools you really need are yourself and the deep power of belief. Magic is all around us, and Wiccans carve out their own practices and learn from their coven and the world the best way to honor the God and Goddess. Create what you can by hand to infuse your energy into your tools. Purchasing or making do with like items is perfectly acceptable (especially if an item is particularly difficult to craft!).

ATHAME   An athame is a ceremonial knife. It is often ornate and adorned in imagery that honors their patron or the practice a Wiccan is participating in. Athames are used to cast circles, trace holy symbols in the air, and in severing rituals. Some practices say they should be dull or sharp on one side or both. For safety purposes, a dull double-edged blade would work best.

BESOM   A besom is a bundle of hand-woven twigs or straw used to bring luck or clean ceremonial spaces. It is more commonly known as a "broom," but besom is the proper magical name. This tool can channel both earth and air. Wiccans can craft their own from gathered materials or purchase a besom that is then consecrated and cleansed for magical use. Individual besoms may be crafted and adorned for specific spells and are generally used in purification or cleansing rituals. Placing a broom across the threshold of your dwelling or under your bed can be a good way to channel such energies.

BOLINE Bolines are ritual knives with a curved blade. The point and the curved edge of the blade are ideal for inscribing candles or harvesting/paring down herbs for rituals. The crescent shape of the blade aligns with the Goddess's connection to the moon. A pair of ritual scissors could be a simple replacement for this tool. In some practices, this is simply a white-handled knife.

BOOK OF SHADOWS A store-bought Book of Shadows is fine and wonderful for inspiration, but a key aspect of Wicca is developing a personal Book of Shadows full of rituals, spells, and communion with the Divine. Find a black book, buy an empty journal, or bind your own Book of Shadows and keep all you know of magic within.

CANDLES Candles serve many purposes in Wicca, and they come in many different forms. Candles of different colors and shapes are used as symbols or torches to help guide intentions. They can be tapered, pillar, tea, or novelty shaped, and ceremonially lighting candles serves as a way of casting out the dark and finding paths when we're lost.

CAULDRON Cast-iron cauldrons are excellent for any spells or rituals that involve fire. They can hold incense, simmer tinctures, or be a fire-safe place to burn ritual items. A traditional cast-iron pot, aluminum pot, or pan is a great stand-in for cauldrons, and Pyrex glass pots offer a lovely visual for whatever is brewing in a witch's pot. If igniting items inside your makeshift cauldron, refrain from using Teflon or otherwise lined pots. These tools hold energy.

CHALICE Chalices are cups used in rituals and on altars. They can be ornate or simple, made of wood, metal, stone, or crystal. Different chalices can be used for different spells, or a single chalice might be used and cleansed in between rituals with converse energies. Chalices are often used to drink ceremonial beverages (traditionally red wine, but nonalcoholic beverages like juice or tea work too) and can hold vestiges of the elements (usually earth or water).

HOLY SYMBOL Holy symbols can be drawn on paper, cast in jewelry, or arranged in crystals. The most easily recognizable symbol is the pentagram or the Triple Goddess. Holy symbols often call to Wiccans, and it is normal to be drawn to any number of holy symbols.

INCENSE Censer or burner varieties of incense are used in different ways. Pine might be suitable for the Horned God while the Goddess might prefer sage. The smoke from incense is used to set the circle, to consecrate tools, as a stand-in for the element of air, and can convey the intent of the ritual.

STANG Used predominantly in traditions passed down by Robert Cochrane, a stang is a wand that more closely resembles a phallus. The tip of the stang may be an acorn or a crystal and will often be a longer staff as opposed to a shorter wand.

WAND Modern wands can be handmade or store-bought and often involve a plethora of crystals to help amplify the energy that the caster works most readily with. For the base, seeking out a branch from a living tree and asking the tree to bestow upon you its energy of life is a great place to start. Refrain from picking up a branch or twig that's already on the ground because its connection to the tree's energy has already been severed. When plucking a wand, be sure to ask permission first. Permission will look like a nearly severed branch or a single low-hanging limb. Slim branches or a lack of reachable limbs would be an example of permission denied.

Anatomy of a Ritual

One of the core elements of Wicca is the ceremonial nature of rituals. Different lineages may tweak certain aspects of a ritual, but the bones remain. That being said, none of these practices is written in stone. Wicca has evolved over the decades that it's been practiced formally, and many Wiccans practice magic outside of ceremonial Wiccan rituals. As an experiential religion, Wicca calls for us to go and get our hands dirty (both metaphorically and literally). Some rituals will require every aspect of the elements mentioned below while simpler spells to deepen connection to the Gods might be more easily accessible. As with all practices in this book, the following elements of a ritual are guidelines and only suggestions. Try to keep at least some version of these core elements in your practice to align with the practices of Wiccans who came before you.

PURIFICATION OF THE SPACE AND PARTICIPANTS This means physically and spiritually cleansing the space and the body to make both ready to receive the Gods. Washing the day of the ritual, blessing yourself with saltwater, and donning special ceremonial garb are great ways to physically cleanse yourself. Washing the floorboards, burning incense, and sweeping out stagnant energy with a besom are great ways to cleanse the space. Setting up the altar prior to the ritual and preparing your materials ahead of time are advised.

CASTING THE CIRCLE The circle is the sacred nonphysical temple where you create a home for the Gods on the material plane. Circle rules and casting practices change from tradition to tradition, but you can find circle casting on page 94. It includes calling down the guardians and petitioning the Gods to join you.

CALLING DOWN THE GUARDIANS Sometimes called the elements, guardians, or watchtowers, these points represent the four cardinal directions and are placed or acknowledged in the layout of the pentagram. The guardians build the border of your circle, and therefore construct the walls of your nonphysical temple.

CALLING DOWN THE GODS Once the circle has been cast and the space has been made holy, the Gods may arrive. Welcome them down from their plane and into ours, and honor and thank them for their presence in your circle for the rest of the ritual. Their presence will often feel like a shift in energy. If they don't come right away, be patient and continue to work with them outside of the ritual.

RAISING ENERGY This can be done through dancing around the circle, physically flexing your muscles, chanting, creating friction between your palms, singing, performing or creating art, and otherwise participating in some type of ecstatic revelry toward the Gods. Once the energy is raised, it can be channeled into a cone of power at the apex of your spherical temple. The cone of power is directed to a specific source by the High Priestess of the coven, or the solitary witch who raised the energy. The cone of power is kept in the circle until it is intentionally released.

Vessels

As Wiccans work magic, vessels are ways we hold and contain that magic. A vessel could be a specifically created magical jar, a cup of tea, a bathtub, or the circle itself. It can be purchased new for the specific purpose of holding a spell or it can be a reused item from your household. Power is given to the object through consecration and through the spellwork. Some examples of vessels are satchels, empty liquor bottles, old spice jars, teacups, pillowcases, bathtubs, cooking pots, and shells. When crafting your own spells, get creative!

SPELLCASTING Not all spellcasting needs to be done in the circle, but an excellent way to channel the cone of power is through spellcasting. It directs the energy to a certain cause or goal rather than simply releasing it to seep out wherever it wants.

GROUNDING OR "CAKES AND ALE" Also known as "The Simple Feast," grounding or "Cakes and Ale" is when you can break bread with the Gods and replenish the energy spent working magic.

THANKING AND DISMISSAL OF GUARDIANS AND GODS The Gods will come and go as they please, but a good host always thanks their guests. Releasing the guardians (especially if elements are tied to them) is always advised. Additionally, showing respect for the circle by consciously deconstructing it rather than just strolling out of it will help deepen your relationship with the Divine.

Finally, you'll notice that many of the rituals in this book have a DIY component. This is intentional. Filling in the blanks to craft bespoke rituals rather than formulaically following an itemized list of what to do and how to do it will help you carve out your own Wiccan path.

Note on magic: Most of Wiccan magic is bestowed from the God and Goddess. Turning to them only to ask for things will cause their gifts to grow thin. Try to honor the God and Goddess with your magic regularly and they will be more inclined to lend their power and grant boons.

ALTARS AND SHRINES

Altars are a space for reverence and devotion to the Gods and ways to channel energy for spells. They can evolve as their caretaker's needs and energies change. Shrines are very similar to altars because they are also a place for devotion and reverence to the God and Goddess, but they typically don't change in their makeup or location. Shrines are also usually outside (although they do not have to be) and are used as a space to release ritual materials back into the earth. They are both traditionally made and adorned with natural materials (wood, linen, stone, and metal); artificial materials (nylon and plastic) are avoided. If that's all you have available, it is completely fine. The God and Goddess won't begrudge you for it.

Different lineages and branches of Wicca have different composition rules for altars. As an eclectic Wiccan, listen to the energies of the God and Goddess when establishing a layout for your altar. Many of the witch's tools (see page 85) are used on altars, especially on altars set up inside a sacred circle.

Every altar is unique, and you do not need to go out and purchase any or all of these tools to create an altar to the Divine. If you do have the following items, lay down the altar cloth first and then you can arrange your altar like so:

LEFT	CENTER	RIGHT
Representation of the Goddess (statue, shell, flowers, fruit, or other symbol)	Bell	Representation of the God (statue, small stag, antler, arrow, or other symbol)
White candle for the Goddess	Pentacle	White candle for the God
Cup or chalice	Incense burner	Red candle for fire
Crystals	Libation dish	Athame
Cauldron	Fresh flowers or found objects of the season	Boline (or white-handled knife)
	Small dish of water	Wand
	Small dish of salt	

Wiccans can have as many altars as they want, but a common practice is keeping one altar as a permanent fixture in your place of residence and one that is created and deconstructed for each celebrated esabat and sabbat.

CASTING A CIRCLE

A magic circle is the base for all of Wicca's ritual magic. Casting a circle creates an unbroken barrier between the sacred working space for your magic and the mundanity of the outside world. When we cast a circle, we build a sacred temple for the Gods, a space between worlds where energy can be raised, communion with the Divine can be reached, and precise magic can be worked.

There are many ways to cast a circle, cleanse the space, order the operations when casting a circle, invoke the Divine and the guardians, select altar tools, and place altar orientations. If one methodology calls to you stronger than the rest, use that. If not, experiment and see what works for you and your space as you build this temple to the Divine. Practice and explore, listen to your intuition, and feel for changes in the energy around you as you cast each circle.

The integrity of the circle's border is to be respected to keep its magic within and as a respectful gesture to the Divine. Once the circle is cast, be sure to cut doorways out by drawing lines of energy with a wand, athame, or just your finger and closing them behind you to keep the energy present.

PROCESS

- Use a cord (perhaps your witch's measure, see page 110) to create a perfect circle. Keep the center point of the cord weighted down and draw the border of the circle with chalk on the floor or trace it with a stick in the dirt. Other barriers include flowers, flour, salt, herbs, crystals, or a rope. Most circles for large groups are approximately 9 feet in diameter, but as long as you have room for an altar, yourself, and some space to move around if your form of raising energy involves ecstatic dance, you should be fine.

- Set up your altar at the northernmost point or at the center. Some traditions also put it toward the east, so you're facing the rising sun. See what works for you.

- Begin by cleansing the space before the circle. This can be with incense, by ringing the bell three times, or by flicking saltwater as you walk around the circle's edge.

- Start casting the circle either to the north, east, or the cardinal direction that aligns with the element of your astrological sun sign (see page 71-74). Cast by pointing your athame, wand, or simply your finger in the direction of your choosing and trace the line of the circle desoil (clockwise). Visualize the energy as you cast. Feel the magic more than simply performing the action. Flexing your muscles as you cast the circle can be a physical way to bring energy to the circle.

- Once the barrier is created, call down the four guardians. This can be done by lighting candles set at north, east, south, and west points of the circle, by holding up their elemental representation on your altar, through hand gestures, or simply by pointing and verbally calling them down. A sample incantation for them can be found after the final step.

- The circle is now cast and the altar candles can be lit, the Divine invoked, energy raised, rituals performed, and spellwork done.

I beckon the guardian of the north to come forth.

May your mountains rise to protect this temple of the Gods.

I beckon the guardian of the east to come forth.

May your winds deliver good fortune upon this temple of the Gods.

I beckon the guardian of the south to come forth.

May your fire light our way in this temple of the Gods.

I beckon the guardian of the west to come forth.

May your water nourish this temple of the Gods.

⚬— INVOKING THE GODS —⚬

The space and your spirit have been cleansed, the circle has been cast, and the guardians have been called. Now it's time to invoke the Gods. Calling down the Divine to the temple we build for them in the circle is one way to work with them. Their presence in our circle can often be felt in a sudden chill, an altered outlook, a quiet hum of energy, or a rush of warmth. Though we call down the Gods, they don't always answer, so take note of what actions and reverence piques their interest the most.

Here are sample invocations as you light your altar candles for the Gods. As you learn more about the ways the God and the Goddess present themselves to you, alter the way you call them. For a longer invocation, see Drawing Down the Moon on page 137.

⤙ Incantation ⤚

Lord and Lady of Witches, Great Goddess and God.
I have built this most sacred temple in your honor.
Please grace me with your presence. So mote it be.

Divine Mother and Father, Sacred Masculine and
Sacred Feminine, wise weavers of the cosmos, hear
my prayer. I have cast this circle and drawn this
temple to venerate you and give my thanks. I bid thee
enter so we can revel in your grace and beauty. As
within, so without.

Horned God and Triple Goddess, Witch Lord and
Witch Queen. I beseech the honor of your divine
company at the threshold of this humble holy house
I've constructed in your name. As above, so below.

Stunning Sun, Magnificent Moon, and Earth Mother.
I invite you to enter this temple I've made in your
honor. Walk with me and observe these rites I
perform to celebrate your gifts. So mote it be.

Movement

Clockwise movement, also called desoil or with the sun, is used to invoke or call something to you. It's also seen as a corkscrew upward to the upperworld of the Gods and can be used to make contact with powerful entities.

Counterclockwise movement, also called windershins, moves against the direction of the sun. It's used to banish or cast away things in spellwork and is the spiral staircase downward to the underworld. Windershins movement is used a lot in working with the dead and ancestor veneration.

Moving against either of these motions will not result in a failed spell; it is simply a tool used to channel your intent into your Wicca practice.

RAISING ENERGY

The circle is made primarily for three reasons: as a temple for the Divine, as protection for the Wiccan, and as a way to harness and channel energy. Raising energy can take the form of many things—dancing, leaping, tensing your muscles, performing calisthenics, clapping your hands, breathing exercises, singing, chanting, art, hand motions, you name it. The point of raising energy is to work yourself up into a state of ecstasy for the Gods. It may feel like glee, a sudden urge to smile, or uncontrollable laughter. It may simply be a blissful little thought about how much you love your life flitting across your consciousness.

By performing actions (any that I mentioned, but traditionally chanting, singing, and dancing), energy is raised to a cone of power within the circle. The cone of power directs the energy raised inside the circle to create a cone of protection. Energy can be raised and channeled to a specific purpose through the cone. Usually, spellwork happens after the energy has been raised and grounded, but raising the energy with the implicit goal of directing it as an act of magic through a cone of power is done as well.

GROUNDING

The purpose of grounding is to send any energy that still mills about the circle back into our bodies and back into the earth so that it doesn't affect anyone nearby or the natural energy of your home.

Eating brings us back into our bodies and into the material plane. Sharing this food and drink with the Gods in a libation dish is customary. It is best to source all food and drink locally where it was made with care (or make it yourself as an offering!). The food is usually something simple, like Crescent Esabat Cakes (see page 106) or a loaf of bread with salted butter. Crackers and cookies are also acceptable. Beverages to rehydrate your body should be shared with the Divine in the chalice and can be local wine (or other alcoholic beverage), seasonal fruit juice, or herbal tea from your garden.

Once the feast is consumed, set aside the remaining liquid in the chalice and food in the libation dish to be given to the Gods in a shrine outside. Composting and otherwise disposing of the Gods' portions is also acceptable, but local avian allies would love it if you gave your oat cakes to them in bird feeders.

AFTER THE RITUAL

Any additional spells are cast after the grounding of the simple feast, but they are not always performed in every circle. Once both the cake has been consumed and the magic has been worked, thank the God and Goddess for their patronage and affection and bid them farewell. Express your gratitude to each of the guardians for protecting your circle, working around the circle, beginning in the west and working counterclockwise to the north. Trace the circle by pointing your finger, wand, or athame to its border to disperse the protection of the circle and snuff any candles still burning (ideally with a snuffer or by wetting your fingers rather than blowing them out).

Clean up any stray ritual items, sweep the floor, and relax.

⚮—— INCANTATIONS ——⚮

Words are a rung on the ladder that we use to reach the Divine. Spontaneous incantations and invocations can be a direct message from the Divine, a gentle nudge in a direction that pleases them more. Additionally, chanting something until the words only have energetic meaning is a form of magic. You've turned something with meaning into simply sound.

Words give Wiccans power and are also completely irrelevant to the ritual itself. If you're confused, I think you're starting to get it. There is power in words. It's how we think, how we connect and interact with others, and how we pray. When I say that they're completely irrelevant, I mean that focusing on the specifics can often lead to praying to a process rather than praying to the Gods. Wicca is experiential. Part of that experience is inherently studious and creative; however, in the co-creative relationship we have with the Gods, they often don't mind if we miss a word or speak out of verse. The words have power because we bestow it on them.

Pair chants with easy beats and don't make invocation too difficult to follow. A rhyme is easier to remember and easier to chant. Incantations are a way to help get your brain out of its normal thinking patterns and into a receptive place to receive information from the God and Goddess and work magic.

WORKING WITH DEITIES

What follows are ways to show respect and pay tribute to the Divine while within the circle:

- Holding up your chalice of sacred wine to the Divine first before taking a sip

- Breaking local or homemade bread with them by placing it on a libation dish

- Placing locally grown flowers in fresh water on the altar

- Presenting them with gifts you've found in nature

- Avoiding the use of synthetic materials in the circle

- Remaining present in rituals by leaving your phone outside the circle

- Adding your own personal touches to rituals

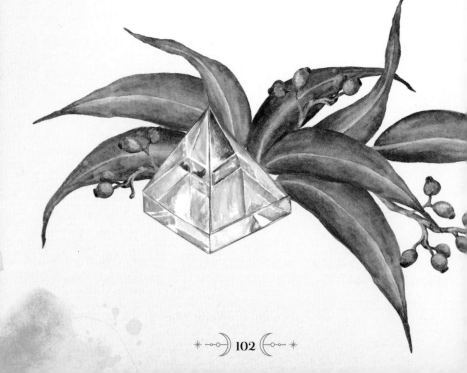

Additionally, here are ways outside of the circle that you can deepen your relationship with them:

- ᖋ Keeping to the sabbats or the esabats

- ᖋ Expressing your utmost gratitude for all of their gifts

- ᖋ Following your passions with wild abandon and presenting them with the fruits of your labor

- ᖋ Being continually curious about the different ways they've manifested

- ᖋ Listening to your intuition regarding feminine and masculine energies that you want to work into your everyday life

- ᖋ Spending time at your altar telling the Divine about the mundanities of your life

- ᖋ Being a steward of the land

- ᖋ Volunteering and providing assistance to all of earth's residents (both human and animal)

As with any relationship, the bond with the Divine is ongoing in a Wiccan's life. Treat them as trusted confidants, treasured friends, and beloved family and tend the relationship regularly.

Wiccan Spells and Rituals

There is magic in the mundane, and Wiccans can make every day fantastical. Whether you're working the big magic of a ritual cast in the circle or weaving the God and Goddess into your day-to-day life, magic is all around you if you simply have the courage to grab it. Cast these spells, make them your own, scribble in the margins, and rewrite incantations. These spells are yours to craft.

Energy Work

CRESCENT ESABAT CAKES

A staple for cakes and ale during rituals, these oat cakes are a perfect offering to the Divine and our ancestors. After rituals, dispose of offerings in bird feeders to give the offering back to the earth. This recipe makes about two dozen small cakes.

Materials

For the cakes
½ cup (110 g) brown sugar

⅓ cup (75 g) butter, at room temperature

1 teaspoon honey

1½ cups (190 g) all-purpose flour

¼ teaspoon baking soda

¼ teaspoon salt

1¼ cups rolled oats

½ teaspoon ground ginger

½ teaspoon ground allspice

1 tablespoon white wine

For the spell
White taper candle

Process

1. For the cakes: Preheat the oven to 350°F (175°C; gas mark 4). Line a baking sheet with parchment paper.
2. In a bowl with an electric beater, beat the brown sugar, butter, and honey on medium speed until fully combined.
3. Sift the flour, baking soda, salt, ginger, and allspice into a separate bowl. Add the oats and whisk to combine.
4. Slowly add the flour mixture to the butter and sugar mixture. Once fully combined, add the white wine, and speak the incantation below.
5. Wrap in plastic and place in the fridge for at least 30 minutes.
6. Roll out the dough between two pieces of parchment paper to ¼ inch thick. Use a butter knife to cut out crescent moons. If it's hard to freehand with a knife, create a template with a sharpie on parchment paper. Place the oat cakes on the prepared baking sheet.
7. Bake for 15 minutes, or until light brown. Allow to cool on a cooling rack for at least 10 minutes.
8. For the spell: Meditate on whatever is waxing or waning in your life. Light the white candle and set one oat cake aside for the Goddess with a small cup of wine.

⟞ Incantation ⟝

Mother moon and Goddess bright,

Though you wax or wane tonight,

With honey sweet and strong wine,

I call upon your power divine.

In your honor we shall feast

To what we grow and what we release.

ANOINTING OIL

Anointing oil is a key element of many Wiccan spells and rituals. You can anoint yourself, candles, or other tools to enhance their magical effects. Crafting your own anointing oil personalizes the energy and weaves your essence into the spells and rituals that they're used for. This magical practice is best performed during a harvest when fresh herbs are in abundance.

Materials

Abundance of fresh herbs (mint, catnip, or basil are all excellent choices)

Small glass mason jar

High-quality olive oil

Process

1. Harvest your herbs from your garden. Thank the Mother Goddess for her bounty and the Sun God for his light.
2. Thoroughly wash and pat dry your herbs with a paper towel.
3. Stuff the herbs into a small jar and then fill it with high-quality olive oil.

4. Shake the bottle every 6 hours or so. You may wish to chant a prayer of thanks while you do so.

5. After a day or so of this, strain the oil through cheesecloth into a clean vessel. Squeeze the herbs in the cheesecloth to ensure that as much oil is released as possible.

6. Restuff the jar with fresh herbs and refill with the oil from your first batch.

7. Repeat the process of shaking and straining the oil at least three times with three batches of fresh herbs.

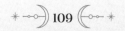

WITCH'S MEASURE

A witch's measure is also known as a "witch's cord" or a "cord of sovereignty." Traditionally, a measure is made by a High Priestess of a coven for a new initiate and then kept by the High Priestess as a symbol of connection to the coven. Your measure can be used to cast circles or as a belt worn in ceremonial garb. You'll see that this rite is fairly similar to the witch's ladder (see page 142) but serves a different purpose.

Materials

9-foot (2.7 m) rope (white or a color that meets the
witch's measure)

Process

1. Gather materials, cleanse and set up the space, and cleanse yourself (see page 88).
2. Cast the circle, invoke the guardians, and call down the God and Goddess (see page 94).
3. Consecrate your rope (see page 112).
4. As you repeat the incantation, start first by tying off a knot at the top of your head.
5. From the top of your rope, measure out the length of your left arm and tie a knot. From the bottom, measure the length of your right arm and tie a knot.
6. Repeat the process for your legs.
7. Repeat the process for your feet.
8. Repeat the process for your hands.
9. Thank the Gods, ground the remaining energy, dismiss the guardians, snuff the candles, and close the circle.

⊰ Incantation ⊱

By knot of one, my rite's begun.

By knot of two, my power to choose.

By knot of three, so mote it be.

By knot of four, bound evermore.

By knot of five, I take a mystic dive.

By knot of six, this cord's affixed.

By knot of seven, the threads are woven.

By knot of eight, I cast this fate.

By knot of nine, connect to the Divine.

CONSECRATION OF TOOLS

Our tools are what we use to connect to and honor the God and Goddess. Consecrating them for a specific magical purpose helps us form and deepen our bond with them outside the realm of the mundane.

Materials

Incense (sage or frankincense would work best)

Candle

Plate of sea salt

Bowl of water

Tool of consecration

Bell (optional)

Process

1. Gather your materials, cleanse the space with sound or smoke before you set up, and then cleanse yourself (see page 88).

2. Cast the circle, light the incense and candle, invoke the guardians, and call down the God and Goddess (see page 94).

3. Take a large pinch of salt and sprinkle it into a bowl of water. Mix using a consecrated athame or wand, or just your finger if you're without either of those tools.

4. Chant the incantation on the following page as you perform the next steps.

    a. Draw the tool to be consecrated through the smoke of the incense (or ring a bell over it).

    b. Draw the tool above the flame of the candle.

    c. Flick saltwater upon your tool.

d. Place the tool on the bed of salt.

5. Ring the bell three times after each consecration if cleansing with sound.

6. Thank the Gods, ground the remaining energy, dismiss the guardians, snuff the candles, and close the circle.

⤙ Incantation ⤚

I invoke the powers of the Divine,
Oh powerful Goddess and God of mine,
I beseech your blessings and power,
To bless this (tool) upon this hour.
Cleanse and purify its energy,
And make the mundane worthy of your divinity.

⊷ — WITCH'S COMPASS — ⥄

A witch's compass is very similar to a circle. A compass is cast in a circle and is used as a way to travel or journey outside the material plane. The setting of the compass will essentially allow you to sit at the threshold without your spirit journeying anywhere. The magic of the circle is woven into the magic of the compass, and protects any entities from entering once the compass is cast. For traveling within the compass, see Treading the Mill, page 122.

Materials

Incense (frankincense, pine, or cedar)

Bowl of salt

Red candle

Bowl of fresh rainwater

Stang, wand, or athame (recommended but optional)

Empty bowl

Bowl of dried herbs or bark (comfrey, dandelion, feverfew, basil, bay leaves, borage, chive, or cinnamon)

Bowl of vinegar

Process

1. Gather the materials, cleanse and set up the space, and cleanse yourself (see page 88).

2. Cast the circle, invoke the guardians, and call down the God and Goddess (see page 94).

3. Light your incense on the altar and center yourself.

4. Invoke the guardians a second time by holding up your offerings for each and reciting the rhyming couplet. Point to each guardian with your stang, wand, or athame.

5. In a bowl, mix the salt and water until they dissolve.

6. Starting at the north, walk the circle in a clockwise direction. Sprinkle and flick the saltwater with your stang, athame, wand, or finger along the edge of the circle as you go and chant the fifth couplet.

7. Return the saltwater to the altar and take up the herb mixture in one hand. Walk the perimeter and sprinkle it as you go, chanting the sixth couplet.
8. Return the herb mixture to the altar and take up the bowl of vinegar in one hand. Sprinkle and flick the vinegar with your stang, athame, wand, or finger along the edge of the circle as you go and chant the seventh couplet.
9. Residing in a liminal space between worlds, meditate or chant to connect to the upperworld or underworld.
10. Thank the Gods, ground the remaining energy, dismiss the guardians, snuff the candles, and close the circle.

⤙ Incantation ⤚

For the earth I gift the salt of life,
Guardian of the north, protect me from strife.

For the air, I gift air from my lungs,
Guardian of the east, mark the rite's begun.

For the fire, a gift burning bright,
Guardian of the south, bless this flight.

For the water, a gift fresh and sweet
Guardian of the west, merry may we meet.

Life and death dance intertwined
I cast this circle for the Divine.

Rebirth comes when seasons end,
I cast this circle for the dead.

Cycles end where they begin,
As without, so within.

SELF-DEDICATION

You cannot self-initiate into a coven. You can, however, self-dedicate yourself to Wicca. This ritual is small but powerful. Words give Wiccans power, so honor yours. Refrain from self-dedicating to Wicca until you're sure you're ready.

Materials

Sea salt scrub

Ceremonial robes or a special outfit

Anointing oil (page 108)

White candle for the God

White candle for the Goddess

Process

1. Gather your materials, cleanse and set up the space, and cleanse yourself (see page 88). Take a shower using an exfoliating scrub. A sea salt scrub is best. Put on your ceremonial outfit.

2. Cast the circle, invoke the guardians, and call down the God and Goddess (see page 94).

3. Anoint one candle with the Horned God symbol and the other with the Triple Goddess symbol (see page 37).

4. Light the candles as you invoke the God and Goddess with the first six lines of the incantation on the following page.

5. Close your eyes and lower your head. Feel out the changing energies. Stretch the limits of your hearing and take note of the vibrations around you.

6. If you're called to raise energy physically, do so now. Otherwise, meditate by focusing on the crown of your head and the connection between the worlds and the Divine. Coming up with a simple chant can also be powerful as you sit in this space. As you feel the shift in energy in the circle, thank the God and Goddess with the last seven lines of the incantation below.

7. Thank the Gods, ground the remaining energy, dismiss the guardians, snuff the candles, and close the circle.

⊸⊱ Incantation ⊰⊷

Wise Mother Goddess,

Brilliant Father God.

I see your face and still don't know you.

Your mysteries draw me in and I submit myself to you.

I dedicate myself to you and the Wiccan path.

Please accept me as your humble servant.

Oh Horned God and Triple Goddess,

I feel the thrum of your power,

Hear the vibrations of your energy,

I see you in me and in the natural world around me.

You bless me with your presence—and I am honored for it.

As above, so below,

As within, so without.

RITUAL BATH

Many of these rites request that you cleanse yourself and your space. Any cleansing with saltwater, sound, or smoke will do, and most covens usually just rinse their bodies before casting the circle. For important rituals, herbs can be added to this bath, which can imbue you with extra energy from nature.

Materials

- ¼ cup Epsom salts
- Assortment of cleansing herbs (peppermint, lemongrass, basil, fennel, hyssop, lavender, mint, rosemary, thyme)
- Petals from local seasonal flowers (or just rose petals)
- Fresh seasonal fruit (slices of apples or oranges)
- Cheesecloth or mesh strainer

Process

1. Run a hot bath and add the salts to the running water.
2. As the tub fills, intentionally add the herbs, flowers, and fruits to your bath.
3. The salts will cleanse and the added herbs, fruits, and flowers will enhance your energy for your ritual. You can make a small satchel of your desired herbs with a cheesecloth and throw it in the tub like a tea bag, or you can leave everything loose.
4. If a cheesecloth isn't used, place a mesh strainer over the drain to collect all the herbs after you pull the plug on the tub.
5. Epsom salts should NOT be used in the garden and can be destructive in compost, so dispose of your organic material in the trash.

Divine Rites

WICCAN NOVENA

A novena is a prayer that lasts for nine days. A consistent prayer is an excellent way to deepen your connection to the Gods. A novena can be used to express gratitude, request assistance on specific matters, or as an affirmation of the self. If exclusively seeking to connect deeper with the God and Goddess, a novena can be used to keep an easy schedule. For a less formal way of splicing the novena into your everyday life, a circle does not have to be cast and you can busy yourself with something else as the candle burns.

Materials

   White seven-day pillar candle

   Prayer beads (optional)

   Representation of the God or Goddess (optional)

Process

1. Mark eight even lines on your votive pillar candle. These will be a measure of how long you should have the candle lit for each of the nine days of the novena.
2. Cleanse the space, cleanse yourself, cast the circle, and invoke the Gods.
3. Light your candle. Hold prayer beads and/or a symbol of the God and/or Goddess in your hands, if desired.

(continued)

4. Chant your request or affirmation aloud at least nine times in front of it. Repeat it in your head until the candle burns down to the first mark. Snuff the candle with a snuffer or by wetting your fingers and snuffing it that way.
5. Thank the Gods, ground the remaining energy, dismiss the guardians, snuff the candles, and close the circle.
6. Repeat this process at the same time every day for nine days.

GUARDIAN MEDITATION

Personalizing your own Wiccan practice will take time and attention. There are many powerful forces at play, and getting to know them is an important aspect of mastering the craft. They may be four nameless guardians, raised to guardian status by the Divine. This guardian meditation will help you connect with the four guardians.

Materials

Bowl of saltwater

Comfortable cushion

Compass

Representation of earth (bowl of salt or earth, pentacle, living plant, and/ or white candle)

Representation of air (incense, bell, fallen leaves, and/or white candle)

Representation of fire (candle, hot peppers, cauldron, and/ or white candle)

Representation of water (bowl of water, seashell, chalice, and/or white candle

Process

1. Prior to this ritual, research the different representations for the four guardians. Take notes in your Book of Shadows.

2. To begin the meditation, cleanse the space by sprinkling saltwater in your meditation area. Place your cushion in the center of your room. Ideally, this will be the room that you will be performing most of your rituals in.

3. Use a compass to find north. About 2 feet (61 cm) away, place the representation of earth.

4. Physically turn your body 90 degrees to find true east. About 2 feet (61 cm)t away, place your representation of air.

5. Physically turn your body 90 degrees to find true south. About 2 feet (61 cm) away, place your representation of fire.

6. Face north and greet the guardian. With a soft focus look at your representation of this guardian. Inhale to a count of three, pause for a count of three, then exhale to a count of three. Continue as you let your mind wander. What does this representation mean for you? How does it manifest in other aspects of your life?

7. Physically turn your body 90 degrees to find true east. About 2 feet (61 cm) away, place your representation of water. Repeat step 6.

8. Physically turn your body 90 degrees to find true south. About 2 feet (61 cm) away, place your representation of fire. Repeat step 6.

9. Physically turn your body 90 degrees to find true west. About 2 feet (61 cm) away, place your representation of water. Repeat step 6.

10. After the meditation, snuff any candles if they haven't burned all the way down yet.

TREADING THE MILL

Popularized by Robert Cochrane, treading the mill is a way to enter a trance state, raise energy in the circle, and open yourself up to communion with the Gods. It is usually done within the witch's compass (see page 114) and can be used to ascend to the upperworld to meet the God and Goddess on their plane or to descend into the underworld and commune with the dead.

Note: Practice this with caution and refrain from pushing yourself too hard and becoming light-headed.

Materials

Compass materials (see page 114)

Stang or wand

Cakes and ale (see page 91)

Process

1. Gather your materials, cleanse and set up the space, and cleanse yourself (see page 88).
2. Cast the circle, invoke the guardians, and call down the God and Goddess (see page 94).
3. Cast the witch's compass (see page 114).
4. Find a focal point at the center of your circle raised in the air. You can hang a stang or wand from the ceiling or a tree branch if this serves you.
5. Walk loosely around the perimeter of the circle. Walk desoil (clockwise) to reach the Gods and windershins (counterclockwise) to travel into the underworld.

6. Hold your left arm parallel to the floor and look over your left shoulder. Close your right eye (or the eye facing out of the circle) and cover it with your right hand. Raise your left eye to the peak of your cone of power. Point your left hand down toward the center of your circle.

7. Keep a rhythm while you walk and occasionally skip a step so that it doesn't feel too rigid. Chant a couplet while you walk the circle (there are a few below to get you started, but making up your own will make it more personal), and spin if you're sure of your balance.

8. Once you're done, fall to the floor exhausted. Energy has been raised and communion with the Gods or spirits is possible.

9. Thank the Gods, ground the remaining energy with cakes and ale, dismiss the guardians, snuff the candles, and close the circle.

⤙ Incantation ⤚

Upper, under, over earth,
Endless cycle of death and rebirth.

Travelers meet and love well met.
Seek to find, get what you get.

Earth, air, fire and water,
Turn the wheel and journey over.

Sabbat Rites

YULE SIMMER POT

Burning a Yule log is a traditional way to celebrate the season. However, many modern homes do not have fireplaces to burn them in, so a simmer pot is a bit more accessible. Intention matters more than tools here, so your simmer pot can be a consecrated kitchen pot, a proper cauldron, or a small pot warmed by tea lights.

Materials

Simmer pot

A collection of aromatic organic material:

> 3-inch (7.5 cm) branch of evergreen (pine, juniper, cedar, or rosemary)
>
> 3 teaspoons spices (cinnamon, ginger, cloves, and bay leaves)
>
> 3 slices of fruits (citrus and apple)

White, red, and/or green candles for your altar

Cakes and ale (see page 91)

Process

1. The night before Yule, consecrate your pot. You don't have to do a full circle for it because it will be part of the circle later, but flicking it with saltwater or running it over incense smoke the night before will do.

2. On the stovetop, add all your collected ingredients to the simmer pot and fill three-quarters with water. It can be a small smattering of the aromatic materials listed or a little bit of all if you can find them.

3. As soon as you wake up, set the simmer pot. It doesn't have to be lit all day, but make sure it's lit when you wake, at noon, and at sunset.

4. Gather materials for the circle (spoon out a bowl of your simmered liquid onto your altar), cleanse and set up the space, and cleanse yourself (see page 88).

5. Cast the circle, invoke the guardians, and call down the God and Goddess (see page 94).

6. Walk the circle with your simmer liquid, flicking it toward the four guardians as you walk the circle three times, chanting one line of the incantation below for each pass.

7. Raise the energy, participate in cakes and ale, and perform any other magical rites now (optional).

8. Thank the Gods, ground the remaining energy, dismiss the guardians, snuff the candles, and close the circle.

9. Give any desserts back to the earth in an outdoor shrine or in a bird feeder.

⊰ Incantation ⊱

Through darkest night, all will be right.

Blessed be both sides of harmony.

With hope and mirth, we celebrate rebirth.

OSTARA SEED AND GARDEN BLESSING

The beauty of spring is in full bloom for Ostara, and it is a prime time to incorporate earth magic into Wiccan rituals to celebrate the Mother Earth aspect of the Goddess. I've made suggestions for easy-to-grow seeds, but research the best types of seeds to plant at this time in your area. Different climates dictate different growing seasons.

Materials

Fertile soil

Late spring or early summer seeds (nasturtium, forget-me-nots, pansies, sunflowers, and zinnias are all easy to grow)

Watering can full of water

Pot

Green candles for your altar

Process

1. Gather your materials, cleanse and set up the space, and cleanse yourself (see page 88).
2. Cast the circle, invoke the guardians, and call down the God and Goddess (see page 94).
3. Present the Divine with the earth, seeds, and water. Plant the seeds in the pot and water them, and then present it a final time. Beseech the Gods for their blessing with the incantation on the following page as you present each offering.
4. Thank the Gods, ground the remaining energy, dismiss the guardians, snuff the candles, and close the circle.

5. Place the blessed plant either in your garden or on a sunny windowsill. Tend it and thank the Gods every time you nurture it and watch it grow. The energy of this blessed plant will spur on the growth of other plants around it.

⊰ Incantation ⊱

Goddess of the flowering spring, bless this earth so that it may feed our harvest.

Most radiant God of the sun, bless these seeds so that they may grow and greenify all that your light touches.

Goddess of flowing waters and our lifeblood, bless this water so that it can nourish new sprouts.

God of fertility, bless these seeds so that they may grow and flower in your light.

❧ — BELTANE MINI MAYPOLE — ☙

Traditionally, a maypole is a celebration involving many people, but this ritual will help a solo practitioner celebrate the magic of weaving a maypole on their own. If it's possible to complete this ritual outside, do so to channel the wild power of nature into your maypole.

Materials

Scissors
3 ribbons
Dowel rod

May flowers, freshly plucked (any from your garden will do, and dandelions are easy to come by if you're not growing flowers)
2 thumbtacks

Process

1. Preparing your mini maypole: With scissors, cut the ribbons to be two and a half times longer than your dowel rod. Hold the dowel upright and lay ribbons on top of it so that the ends fall evenly crisscrossed. Pick the head of a sturdy flower and pin the center of the flower with one thumbtack above the ribbons to the dowel to hold all of them in place. This should let six ribbons fall loosely around the dowel. Save the second thumbtack for the end of the ritual.

2. Ritual: Gather your materials, cleanse and set up the space, and cleanse yourself (see page 88).

3. Cast the circle, invoke the guardians, and call down the God and Goddess (see page 94).

4. Wish the God and Goddess a happy union and raise physical energy to their joy. Play happy music in the background. Dance around the circle and practice therapeutic laughter.

5. Before you are thoroughly exhausted, either sit and braid the ribbons down your maypole or take an easy lilting walk around the circle. Chant the following incantation while you do so. Once you weave your maypole to the bottom of the dowel, pin the bottom with the thumbtack.

6. Thank the Gods, ground the remaining energy, dismiss the guardians, snuff the candles, and close the circle.

7. Place the maypole on your altar or in your garden. You could also deconstruct your maypole and hang the ribbons in trees by your house.

⌁ Incantation ⌁

A divine dance of life and ardent love
Blessed by those below and those above,
Honorable May Queen and May King,
We celebrate your union and the joy it brings.

LITHA BLESSING AND BURNING

At times of abundance, when many paths are open to us, this ritual can mark the fork in the crossroads. We can choose what to burn away from us and what seeds we want to grow. Gather energy from nature to enhance the magic of this ritual and weave in some dreamwork to help you carve your path forward.

Materials

7 found flowers (ideally from your garden or in the wild)

Vase of water

White satchel

Fire-safe cauldron

Process

1. Gathering the flowers: When gathering materials from nature, it is always important to ask for permission. I can see you rolling your eyes and asking how flowers can acquiesce to your requests if they can't speak. This is a chance to learn how to communicate with nature without words. Permission to take a flower may look like a field of abundant blooms, a partially crushed stem, or a bud creeping onto the path. Also, be aware of your local foraging laws. Many national and state parks forbid foraging protected native plants. Respecting the conservation of natural resources is respecting the gifts of the God and Goddess. Collecting seven flowers from nature is an ideal way to gather the raw power of summer; however, if the wildflowers are few and far between, and you don't have any ready in your own garden, purchasing flowers is completely acceptable. Do some additional research on the flowers you collect to deepen your connection to this ritual.

2. Shake out the flowers gently and let them sit out on a windowsill in a vase of water for at least one day before the ritual.

3. Ritual: Gather your materials, cleanse and set up the space, and cleanse yourself (see page 88).

4. Cast the circle, invoke the guardians, and call down the God and Goddess (see page 94).

5. Place the vase of flowers at the center of your altar, and place the satchel on the right and the cauldron on the left. Alternate placing flower heads in the satchel and in the cauldron. For every flower head placed in the cauldron, name something you'd like to shed. For every flower head placed in the satchel, name something you'd like to affirm or grow. Try to place three flowers in the cauldron and three in the satchel, leaving the final flower for the Gods. Alternatively, if there is more that you'd like to grow or get rid of, pluck the petals off instead of placing the flower head in the cauldron and satchel. Concentrate on the things you'd like to release as you burn the flowers in the cauldron.

6. Thank the Gods, ground the remaining energy, dismiss the guardians, snuff the candles, and close the circle.

7. Dispose of ashes outside after the ritual is over. Place the satchel under your pillow for dreams to guide you toward your manifestation. After one night, dispose of the flowers outside and wash the satchel for future use.

LUGHNASADH
BREAKING OF BREAD

The grain harvest should not be wanting for bread. Bake a special loaf or visit your local farmers' market or bakery to find a bread baked with care by someone who lives on the land. Celebrants at Lughnasadh festivals in the past threw bread over their shoulders as an offering to predators in hopes that they wouldn't attack their livestock before the final harvest. This ritual will be a way to show your gratitude to the earth that feeds us and the creatures we share it with.

Materials

Loaf of bread (from a local bakery or baked fresh by your own hand)

Libation bowl

Fire-safe cauldron

Yellow, gold, or orange candle for your altar

Sunflower for your altar

Process

1. Gather your materials, cleanse and set up the space, and cleanse yourself (see page 88).
2. Cast the circle, invoke the guardians, and call down the God and Goddess (see page 94).
3. Hold the bread high above your head and invoke the first three lines of the following incantation.
4. Break off a piece and give it to the guardian of the north (earth) and say the fourth line.
5. Break off a piece and give it to the guardian of the east (air) and say the fifth line.
6. Break off a piece and give it to the guardian of the south (fire) and say the sixth line.

7. Break off a piece and give it to the guardian of the west (water) and say the seventh line.
8. Break off a piece and place it in your libation bowl for the Gods and the guardian of the spirit and say the eighth line. Keep one final piece for yourself.
9. Say the final two lines and eat your piece of bread.
10. Thank the Gods, ground the remaining energy, dismiss the guardians, snuff the candles, and close the circle.
11. Bring the bread given to the guardians to four corners of your house where they'll be safe to reside for a few days. Let the four pieces of bread sit in the four corners for 24 hours to one week. Give the offerings back to the earth by either feeding it to the ducks or placing it in an outdoor shrine or bird feeder. If you attend any bonfires, throw the bread upon the pyre.

❈ Incantation ❈

Luminous Lugh, bright and brilliant

We give thanks for the bounty you have laid in our fields,

We reap the gilded grain that it yields and submit this offering.

To the north, for stability and abundance.

To the east, for inspiration and communication.

To the south, for courage and passion.

To the west, for forgiveness and consistent compassion.

To the spirit, for balance and binding.

Happy and healthy golden harvest,

Blessed be.

SAMHAIN DUMB SUPPER

A dumb supper or dumb dinner is usually performed at times when the veil between the living and the dead is the thinnest. For this ritual, you may want to cast your circle around a dinner table.

Materials

Desserts or Crescent Esabat Cakes (page 106)

A rich meal with protein and fats

Libation dish for the God and Goddess and each of the dead

Chalice or cup for the God and Goddess and each of the dead

White candle for the God and Goddess and each of the dead

Bread

Wine

Process

1. Make desserts ahead of time. Just prior to casting the circle, craft a hot meal that fits the tastes of the invited dead.

2. In addition to a libation dish and chalice for the God and Goddess, set the table for as many beloved, mighty, and nameless dead as you'd like to invite. I'd recommend no more than three of one type or one of each so that you can commune with each of them personally. Add a candle for each guest.

3. Gather the meal, cleanse and set up the space, and cleanse yourself (see page 88).

4. Cast the circle, invoke the guardians, and call down the God and Goddess (see page 94).

5. Invoke the God and Goddess. Thank them for their love and guidance as you light their candle.

6. Cut a door in your circle and say the following invocation aloud. Incorporate the names of your dead into the invocation as you light each of their candles. Close the circle once the dead have entered.

7. Serve the dessert first in the God and Goddess's libation dishes, then serve a small portion of dessert for the rest of the honored dead on their dishes. Serve yourself dessert last.

8. Feast and commune with the dead. Share any letters you've written them or say kind words as you eat. Move through the courses backward, breaking the bread with your guests last. Be sure to serve the Divine first, then the dead, and then yourself.

9. Thank the Gods, thank the guests, and say goodbye.

10. Ground the remaining energy, dismiss the guardians, and close the circle.

11. Give the desserts back to the earth in an outdoor shrine or in a bird feeder.

⤙ Incantation ⤚

*Beloved dead of flesh and bone, I welcome you
to a seat at my table.*

I bestow sweet cakes first, a well-deserved dessert.

I bestow wine for your merrymaking.

*I welcome you, dear heart, to join me as
you did in life,*

I honor you with love and remembrance.

*Mighty dead, powerful and enlightened, I welcome
you to a seat at my table.*

I bestow sweet cakes first, a well-deserved dessert.

I bestow wine for your merrymaking.

*I welcome you, wise one, to see the reach
of your influence,*

I honor you with reverence and revelry.

*Nameless dead, many and forgotten, I welcome you
to a seat at my table.*

I bestow sweet cakes first, a well-deserved dessert.

I bestow wine for your merrymaking.

*I welcome you, dear spirit, to take part in the
joys of life.*

I honor you with compassion and dignity

Moon Rites

DRAWING DOWN THE MOON

This is a rite for full moons when the Goddess is at the peak of her power. Drawing down the moon calls her close to home.

Materials

Dark-bottomed shallow circular bowl filled with water

White candle (taper or pillar)

Process

1. Gather your materials, cleanse and set up the space, and cleanse yourself (see page 88).

2. Cast the circle, invoke the guardians, and call down the God and Goddess (see page 94).

3. Keep your bowl below eye level. Light the candle and hold it high.

4. Invoke the Goddess with revery. The Goddess goes by many names. You'll learn her many forms as you practice, and as she reveals parts of herself to you, you can spontaneously draw down the moon in a way that reflects your own intimate relationship. Until you feel comfortable drawing down the Goddess on your own, you can read the incantation below. The second half of the incantation is spoken as the Goddess speaks through you.

5. If you choose to write your own incantation, use the following formula: Begin by calling her down by all of her names and call her into yourself.

(continued)

6. Stand in the Goddess position, with legs and arms splayed out wide towards the ground and head tilted back towards the sky, and praise her for the aspects that you most cherish. Pay compliments to her strengths, express gratitude for her gifts, and acknowledge her omniscience.

7. Raise energy through ecstatic dance, music, or other way to honor the Gods.

8. Thank the Gods, ground the remaining energy, dismiss the guardians, snuff the candles, and close the circle.

⊸ Incantation ⊷

Great Goddess, Feminine Divine, Lady of the Moon with many faces, I invoke you by Artemis, by Hekate, by Persephone, to descend upon your humble servant, to speak through my lips, feel through my heart, and bask in my love.

Dear one whom I guard and guide. I am your Maiden of the sea and stars, Mother of the fertile earth, wizened Crone of ages passed. Your honor of the Witch Queen on this full moon with the utmost reverence and joy calls me down. You feel my touch on a summer's breeze, see my work in the rooting of seeds, and taste my compassion in the salt of your tears. My mysteries are many, but seek and you shall find what you need. Every beginning is an end, and there is mirth and sorrow to be found in both. Dance in the liminal space where I am all. Dredge deep your life and I will drink with you. I am life, I am death, I am love, and I am with you. Be true to yourself and I will be true to you.

NEW MOON BLACK MIRROR

Any form of divination will be enhanced in the new moon, but using a dark disk to aid divination symbolically pays homage to the mysterious dark moon. Also known as a witch mirror, it can be used to scry at any time after this, new moon or not.

Materials

Black candle

Small mirror

Anointing oil (see page 108)
  or essential oil of choice

Black acrylic paint

Paintbrush (optional)

Process

1. Gather your materials.
2. Light the black candle. Anoint your mirror with the shape of the pentagram with your anointing oil.
3. Paint one half of your mirror with the black paint. It can be even, ridged, goopy, swirling, abstract, or include symbols. You can use a paintbrush or paint with your fingers.
4. Let the mirror sit out on your altar to dry. Depending on how much paint you used, this may take some time.
5. Once dry, anoint the mirror with oil in the shape of a pentagram again. Before you look at it, bring an open-ended question to mind. Yes-or-no answers usually do not translate in divination.
6. With the question at the forefront of your mind, and your consciousness focused on your third eye, observe the black side of the mirror with a soft gaze. Let your vision swim and pull out abstract images. What jumps out at you? Record your impressions and maybe draw any of the symbols in your Book of Shadows.

DARK MOON DREAMING

While this moon magic is specifically for the new moon, starting this rite at the beginning of the waning moon will yield the best results. This satchel facilitates "flying" or a dream flight with psychic visions.

Materials

Dried lavender

Dried bay leaves

Dried mugwort

Dried mullein

Satchel

Silver ribbon (optional)

Dream journal

Pen

Process

1. On the first day of the waning gibbous moon, add a tablespoon of all the dried herbs to the satchel. At sunset, hold your dream satchel to the sky and humbly request that the Crone bless your dreams. Tie the satchel tightly, maybe even tying an extra length of silver ribbon around it.

2. Place the satchel inside your pillowcase on the side away from your head.

3. Every morning of the waxing moon, record your dreams in vivid detail. Write three pages, if you can.

4. At the next new moon, review your dream journal. Look for common themes and images. See if anything or anyone feels particularly intriguing. Dive into folklore around these images.

⚮— FULL MOON WATER —⚮

If a full Drawing Down the Moon ritual (see page 137) isn't possible, make some moon water and thank the Goddess when you use it to strengthen your relationship to the Divine.

Materials

Label

Pen or marker

Silver ribbon

Clear glass jar

Quartz crystal (optional)

Process

1. Create a label for the jar, charting the date of the full moon and other details that may pertain to it, such as the season, the astrological correspondence of the moon at the time, and the month of the moon if these hold any particular significance to you.
2. String the silver ribbon through the label and tie it around the neck of the jar.
3. Drop the quartz into the jar to enhance the power and fill the jar with water.
4. Leave the jar outside or on a windowsill where it can catch the light of the full moon.
5. Use the moon water to water your garden or houseplants, or as the water on your altar for your next sabbat or esabat.

Drawing Rites

WITCH'S LADDER

A witch's ladder is a way Wiccans can harness and keep the magic raised in a circle. The stored energy can be released when a burst is needed later. Witch's ladders have been done many times before and the rhyming of the invocation is created and recreated over and over again, so feel free to swap out any lines that don't work for you.

Materials

At least 1 foot (30 cm) of rope, embroidery floss, yarn, or other thread

Process

1. Gather your materials, cleanse and set up the space, and cleanse yourself (see page 88).
2. Cast the circle, invoke the guardians, and call down the God and Goddess (see page 94).
3. Consecrate your rope (see page 112).
4. When tying each knot, chant the rhyme that corresponds to the numbered knot you're tying.
5. Tie the first knot in the middle. Tie the second at the top. Tie the third at the bottom.
6. Halfway between the first and second knot, tie the fourth. Between the first and third knot, tie the fifth.
7. Starting at the top, tie a knot between each of the existing knots for a count of nine.

8. Thank the Gods, ground the remaining energy, dismiss the guardians, snuff the candles, and close the circle.
9. When untying the knots to release their power, untie them in the same order they were tied.

⇥ Incantation ⇤

By knot of one, this spell's begun.

By knot of two, this power will do.

By knot of three, so mote it be.

By knot of four, magic at its core.

By knot of five, this spell will thrive.

By knot of six, power held betwixt.

By knot of seven, the energy given.

By knot of eight, cast to create.

By knot of nine, blessed by the Divine.

CANDLE FOR CONFIDENCE

Invoking the power of fire through candle magic can be a powerful way to incite passion and light a spark. When working with candles, especially seven-day candles that take a while to burn down, snuff them either by wetting your fingers and pinching the wick or by using a candle snuffer. This ritual does not need to be done in the circle.

Materials

Incense (optional)

Athame, boline, or toothpick

Orange or yellow candle

Anointing oil (see page 108)

Bell

Process

1. Gather your materials and light the incense (if using).

2. With caution, use your athame, boline, or a toothpick to carve your name into the candle vertically. Mark two to six lines evenly down the length of the candle depending on how many days you plan to do this ritual.

3. Dab anointing oil on your index fingers and thumbs. In a clockwise corkscrew motion, anoint the candle from the base to the wick. Note: Do *not* anoint the wick itself.

4. Take your time anointing the candle and massage the oil into the grooves of your name. Imagine what a more confident version of yourself would look and act like. How would you speak? How would you act? How's your posture? What kind of thoughts does confident you have? Really visualize a confident you.

5. Draw the candle over the smoke of the incense, turning it to bless the entire candle. Place your candle in its holder and ring the bell three times at the points of a triangle around your candle.
6. Light the candle and continue to visualize your most confident self.
7. Burn to your marked line and snuff the candle. Leave it on your altar and repeat this ritual three to seven nights in a row.

SPELL JAR FOR ABUNDANCE

Recycle old spice jars or small bottles into a magical talisman for a multitude of purposes. This jar is meant to bring abundance to your life. This can be in the form of finances, time, companionship, work, or any other area of your life that you're looking to fill up. Personalize this jar however you see fit.

Materials

Small jar with a lid or cork

Incense or bell

Paper and pen

Assortment of herbs, dried or fresh (marigold for attraction, lavender for happiness, allspice for fortune, nutmeg for money, cinnamon for success, moonwort for prosperity, dandelion for wishes)

Drop of honey

A dish or tray to catch stray wax

Short green candle (no taller than 8 inches, or 20 cm)

Process

1. Gather your materials and bless the jar with smoke or sound (see page 88).
2. On a small piece of paper, write the areas in your life that you want to bring abundance to. Keep it simple: only one word or phrase.
3. Roll up the paper and slide it into the jar.
4. Take pinches of each of the dried or fresh herbs you'd like to add to your spell jar. As you add each pinch, say aloud what they are for.

5. Once the jar is about three-quarters full of herbs, add a drop of honey for attraction.

6. Close the jar and gently shake it, repeating what each of the herbs is for. Place the jar on a dish to catch the candle wax.

7. Melt some of the wax on the bottom of the candle and place it on the top of your jar. Light the candle and let it burn down to seal the top in wax. Burn the whole candle, even if it takes several sittings to do so.

8. Once complete, carry the jar with you in a satchel or keep it on your altar. Once you feel its magic waning, thank the talisman for the gifts it granted and break the wax seal. Bury, burn, or otherwise dispose of the contents. Wash and reuse or recycle the jar.

⋅≺ Incantation ≻⋅

Marigold to magnetize

Lavender for happiness

Allspice for fortune

Nutmeg for money

Cinnamon for success

Moonwort for prosperity

Dandelion for granted wishes

Banishing Rites

LAYING DOWN SIMPLE WARDS

Magic is the art of attracting, and sometimes your work will draw in unwanted attention. Wards protect your home from negative energy, hexes, and unwanted visitors that come sniffing around. They lose their power over time, so renew your wards once a year, ideally at the end of September/beginning of October to prep for the time of year when the space between worlds is the thinnest. Wards can be laid after casting the circle by cutting a door or you can lay them yourself.

Materials

Bowl of salt

Bowl of water

Athame (optional)

Bell

Incense and censer
  (sandalwood for peace and
  grounding, thyme to ward
  off negativity, or sage for
  protection)

Process

1. Gather your raw materials, cleanse and set up the space, and cleanse yourself (see page 88).

2. Cast the circle, invoke the guardians, and call down the God and Goddess (see page 94).

3. Add heavy pinches of salt to the bowl of water. Mix it with your athame or your finger.

4. Cut a door in your circle with your finger or athame. Holster your athame on your belt if using.

5. Attach the bell to your finger or wrist of your right hand. Hold the censer in your right hand.

6. Hold the bowl of saltwater in your left hand. Walk out of the circle through the hole you cut. Close it again by drawing a pentagram with your incense hand.

7. Moving clockwise around the house, place the bowl and incense by every ingress/egress. Anoint all windows and doors, dipping your finger into the saltwater from the bowl and then using it to draw a pentagram. Ring the bell seven times, and then move on to the next window or doorway.

8. Once you've warded all of your windows and doors, return to the circle.

9. Thank the Gods, ground the remaining energy, dismiss the guardians, snuff the candles, and close the circle.

WITCH BOTTLE TO SHIELD FROM HARM

Wiccan spell jars are talismans of harnessed energy. Some of them harness the gentle protection of powerful items, and others use positive energy to ward off negative energy. Adding a bit of yourself will tie you to the protection of the bottle, and while Wiccans of the past have used blood and urine, spit or hair will bind the bottle to you just as well.

Materials

- Small glass bottle (spice jars work well)
- Incense or bell
- Protective gardening gloves
- Collected sharp objects
- Dish or tray to catch wax
- Black candle approximately the same height as your bottle

Process

1. Gather your materials and bless the jar with smoke or sound (see page 88).

2. Keep your bottle and your protective gardening gloves on your person. Carefully collect any sharp objects in your small bottle. This can be loose nails or screws, broken glass or mirrors, or anything else that has jagged edges.

3. When the jar is full, spit into it if adding a 'piece of yourself,' close the lid. Place it on a dish to catch melting the candle wax.

4. Melt some of the wax on the bottom of the candle and place it on the top of your jar. Light the candle and let it burn down to seal the top in wax. Speak the incantation below as the candle burns.

5. Bury the jar 7 inches (18 cm) underground.

⊰ Incantation ⊱

As without, so within.

I invoke the Triple Goddess and the Horned God to protect me from harm.

I beseech the divine to hold my wards.

Blessed be.

Acknowledgments

I'd like to offer a deep and heartfelt thanks to the marvelous team at Wellfleet for the opportunity to write about Wicca. The team's dedication to supplying new seekers with knowledge is truly a gift. Amy Lyons, your kind and gentle encouragement as we teased out the mysteries of Wicca was a wonderful companion. Cara Donaldson and Rage Kindelsperger, you have my utmost gratitude for the opportunity to continue to bring magic into the world.

Blessed be the friends that gifted their wisdom and loaned their books. A special tip of the hat to the libraries that hold sacred texts that help build a budding witch's Book of Shadows.

An additional thanks to my doting partner, who made sure I drank water while writing haloed in clouds of incense. The world would be much less enchanting without you.

A final and most humble thanks to the Divine and their gentle hand of guidance, as well as the magical readers who make books like this possible.

Resources and References

WEBSITES

American Folkloric Witchcraft: http://afwcraft.blogspot.com
Archived blog content with well researched posts on rituals and
Wiccan lore.

Celtic Connection: https://wicca.com
One of the oldest and largest Wicca, Witchcraft, and Pagan sites
about magical lifestyles.

Almanac: www.almanac.com/topics/astronomy/moon
This particular link is a good place to start looking at moons, but
Almanac.com explains many natural phenomena and provides up-
to-date records for the natural world.

Infinite Beyond: www.infinite-beyond.com
Christopher Orapello and Tara-Love Maguire's internet resource
for the Blacktree Coven's brand of eclectic Wicca.

Learn Religions: www.learnreligions.com
Internet archive for all major and minor religions and deities.

Mandragora Magika: www.mandragoramagika.com
A Wiccan Pagan Network with pagan resources and media as well
as coven search tools.

Pagan Library: www.paganlibrary.com
Public domain archive of source materials for Wiccans and
Pagans alike.

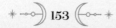

Patheos: www.patheos.com
Patheos is a hub for many religious and spiritual blogs. The
following links are the professional blogs of prominent figures in
the Wiccan community.

**By Athame and Stang: www.patheos.com/blogs/
byathameandstang/author/keldend**
Historical and folkloric witchcraft writer and content creator
Kelden Mercury.

**For Puck's Sake: www.patheos.com/blogs/matauryn/author/
mauryn**
Mat Auryn's a professional psychic who has written many books,
periodicals, and worked with many other well known Witches.

**Raise the Horns: www.patheos.com/blogs/panmankey/author/
jmankey**
Jason Mankey is a prolific pagan writer and his blog is an
excellent source of deity information and Wiccan holidays.

Internet Sacred Texts Archive: www.sacred-texts.com
Similar to the Pagan Library, this resource holds a wealth of
public domain sacred texts for Wiccans, including the following:

> **Aradia (or the Gospel of Witches): www.sacred-texts.com/
> pag/aradia**
> Written by Charles G. Leland in 1899, this is a sacred text for
> many Dianic Wiccan practices.

> **Charge of the Goddess: www.sacred-texts.com/bos/
> bos058.htm**
> Doreen Valiente's short but sweet moral code for Wiccans.

The Laws from Lady Sheba: www.sacred-texts.com/bos/bos258.htm
The 162 laws for Wiccans by Lady Sheba are one of the better-known moral codes for Wiccans.

The Old Laws: www.sacred-texts.com/pag/gbos/gbos38.htm
Gerald Gardner's Craft Laws from 1961.

The Wiccan Rede: www.sacred-texts.com/bos/bos312.htm
Gwen Thompson's poem "Rede of the Wiccan."

Spells8: www.spells8.com
Resource for spells, lore, and more for solitary witches and Wiccans.

Thorn Mooney: www.thornthewitch.wordpress.com/
Thorn Mooney is one of the newest yet well-known voices in the Wiccan community.

Wicca Living: www.wiccaliving.com
Lisa Chamberlain's Wiccan wisdom is a great resource for beginners.

PODCASTS

Down at the Crossroads podcast: https://podcasts.apple.com/us/podcast/down-at-the-crossroads-music-magick-paganism/id303483786

Seeking Witchcraft podcast: https://podcasts.apple.com/us/podcast/seeking-witchcraft/id1462656660

BOOKS

Aradia: Gospel of Witches by Charles Leland

Besom, Stang & Sword by Christopher Orapello and
    Tara-Love Maguire

The Complete Art of Witchcraft by Sybil Leek

Eight Sabbats for Witches by Janet Farrar and Stewart Farrar

The Golden Bough by James Frazer

Herbal Magic by Aurora Kane

Living Wicca by Scott Cunningham

The Meaning of Witchcraft by Gerald Brosseau Gardner

New World Witchery by Cory Thomas Hutchenson

The Rebirth of Witchcraft by Doreen Valiente

Solitary Witch by Silver RavenWolf

Traditional Wicca: A Seeker's Guide by Thorn Mooney

Traditional Witchcraft by Gemma Gary

Weaving the Liminal by Laura Tempest Zakroff

The White Goddess by Robert Graves

Wicca: A Guide for the Solitary Practitioner by Scott Cunningham

*Wicca: History, Belief, and Community in Modern Pagan
    Witchcraft* by Ethan Doyle White

Wicca for Life by Raymond Buckland

Witchcraft for Tomorrow by Doreen Valiente

Index